To my fellow lovers of flavor.

Zest by Alexis Taylor

www.makeitwithzest.com

© 2021 Alexis Taylor

hello@makeitwithzest.com

ISBN: 978-0-578-95248-2

ZEST

Simple ways to elevate your favorite foods

ALEXIS TAYLOR

WITH JUSTIN TAYLOR

CONTENTS

THIS BOOK IS FOR YOU

This book is for people who like to cook, and love to eat.

In a world where it seems all recipes must be *quick and easy*, where hero shots of food are posted to social media like a popularity contest, I know there are still those of us who enjoy the process of cooking, and find sitting down to a meal with friends and family to be the most pleasurable part of the day. Not *every* meal, mind you, nor *every* recipe. We live busy lives with myriad responsibilities vying for our attention. But when we have time, we want to create something beautiful. I wrote this book for you. Real recipes that work - some short, some long, all delicious - for when you just want to *make* something.

I was born with a hunger to create food. Before I could walk, I'm told I'd sit on my mother's hip as she made dinner each night, mesmerized by the action from my perch above the counter. By age 8, I insisted on making my own birthday cakes, and still do to this day. It's like a present I give to myself each year, a frosted gift from which I derive the utmost pleasure.

By the time I was in college, I was developing my own recipes, learning by trial, and often error, how to combine ingredients. The flavors weren't all that sophisticated, but neither was I. During sophomore year my roommate invited her parents to dinner in our rather grungy, one-bedroom apartment in Washington, D.C. As she posted up in our galley kitchen, my other roommate and I vacated the space for her family's special evening. I anxiously awaited our opportunity to return. She was following *my* recipe, one that I had made on countless occasions for friends, but this was the first time I had jotted down a recipe for someone *else* to follow; boneless chicken breasts slathered in dijon mustard, sauteed with lots of bell peppers and onions, and finished with a splash of white wine. The suspense was killing me. As I walked through the door, nerves going haywire, immediately I read on their faces the meal was a success. Phew! It was a small win, but one that boosted my confidence, setting the stage for my future.

I knew back then that I longed to be in the kitchen, though culinary school wasn't ever a consideration. I believed, at that time, that all professional cooking happened late at night, and at a frantic pace. As someone whose most productive hours are in the morning, a restaurant's back of the house during dinner service rush was certainly not the place for me. And so, I continued to cook as I could, and travel whenever possible to experience other cuisines. I went on to graduate school, studying my second love, art history. Washington, D.C. was the most amazing place to study art, being home to world renowned museums and galleries, and with access to the Library of Congress. During grad school I interned at Christie's auction house, and planned to move to New York to get a job in their antiquities department after I received my degree. My passion was ancient Roman art and archeology. I've always had a special place in my heart for all things Italian - of course, food included!

Love struck, throwing a major wrench in those plans. I met a boy and put New York on hold. While I was finishing my thesis, I had taken a job at Dean and Deluca in Georgetown. Glorious food was all around me. I was in heaven, except for one thing... my job in catering sales had *nothing* to do with the preparation of food. From my desk on the second floor balcony, I peered down into the store, overlooking the cheese case, the glistening salads, overstuffed sandwiches and decadent baked goods. The "line" where all prepared food was made, was 15 feet from my desk. More often than my boss appreciated, I found myself chatting with the chefs, gaining tips on everything from making salad dressing to searing tuna. I realized then, that was where I wanted to be, cooking for people - not stuck behind a desk.

That guy whom I had fallen in love with, now many years my husband, knew where my heart lay. As I neared my breaking point with catering sales, he came across an article about a trend growing in popularity in the larger cities across America: personal cheffing. Not to be confused with *private chefs*, who work exclusively for one family, *personal chefs* have a number of clients, and prepare meals with instructions for the family to warm or finish. The formula goes like this: Meet with the client to understand their preferences and aversions, prepare a menu for the upcoming service, grocery shop on the morning of, arrive at the client's house with ingredients and equipment, prepare five meals, package and store those meals in the fridge/freezer, clean up, leave reheating or finishing instructions, take the trash out and be on your way like you were never there, save the wonderful aromas left behind. It seemed like a dream. I would get to cook during the day, on my own terms and do the kind of cooking I'm best at - homestyle.

I finished up my thesis and enrolled in a certification course preparing me to own and operate my own personal chef business. In 2002, I founded Cucina Fresca, and with a few referrals I was off and cooking. The market was ripe for personal chef services. Within a few months my schedule was overflowing, and after two years, by the age of 26, I was featured in the Washingtonian Magazine as a top personal chef in the broader D.C. metro area.

Fast forward almost two decades, through a cross-country move, bakery gigs, owning my own chocolate company, and having three kids, here I am, a cookbook author and food blogger, whose favorite place to be is in the kitchen and cooking for those I love. As a mom, many nights I NEED to put dinner on the table lickety-split; but most nights all I *want* to do is to pour a glass of wine, crank the tunes and savor the journey. On those nights - or mornings, as the case may be - the food in this cookbook is the food I want to eat.

My cooking isn't fancy, I'm a home cook and I make what our family and friends like. Sometimes that's a kale salad, and sometimes it's pizza and brownies. Sometimes we crave a steaming bowl of pasta, dusted with fresh parmigiano, and sometimes it's tacos bursting with chilis and the bold flavors of Mexico.

Make it with Zest

No matter the mood, cuisine or time constraints, *everything* I cook is made with ZEST! Although there is a fair amount of citrus zest in my cooking, what I mean by cooking with zest is incorporating that perfect, easily sourced ingredient which makes the dish pop and reach its full potential. Sometimes the star ingredient is overt; often it's weaved into the flavor profile and one wouldn't readily guess its presence. And occasionally making something with zest means using a new and innovative approach. Whatever the form, zest elevates the dish to something that you've heretofore likely not experienced. For each recipe, at the top of the page, I've identified the zest factor so you know what it is that makes the dish special.

It was a wise chef who once said, if food doesn't evolve, it dies. Traditions will always be with us, but day-to-day we don't cook the way of generations past. Reenvisioning is the only way to keep a recipe relevant- which is why you'll see many recognizable dishes in my book, but with a slightly different approach. I'm not talking about trends. Trends come and go, and I try not to get too caught up in them. Instead, I use classic techniques and flavors and infuse them with something novel. To keep food and our taste buds ever expanding, you need to make it with ZEST!

TIPS FROM THE CHEF

MY BASIC INGREDIENTS

SALT: Proper seasoning is vital to the success of a dish. Salt brings out flavor, both sweet and savory alike. I give measurements for every recipe that will get you very close, however, you should always taste your food to dial in the seasoning. I generally moderately salt at the beginning of the recipe, as it draws out the flavor of the ingredients and allows it to meld into the dish, and then finish with seasoning at the end to balance. There is a range of appropriate seasoning between too little and overly salted, and within that range it is a personal preference. The only way to get it right is to taste. The type of salt one uses is incredibly important. I exclusively cook with Morton's coarse kosher salt because I know how it feels in my hands and reacts in a dish. Once you get to know a salt and a chef's recipes, you can stop using measuring spoons and cook by intuition. Until then, use measurements as a guide, always tasting and adjusting. In addition to cooking with salt, certain recipes call for a flaky salt to finish. This is used for texture and flavor. I use Maldon sea salt flakes.

PEPPER: A mill for freshly ground black pepper is a must. Pre-ground black pepper will not empart the same flavor and bite as freshly ground. I use a grinder that has an adjustment allowing for finer and coarser grinds, however, one with a single setting is still a better option.

OLIVE OIL: Good ingredients result in better tasting food. Olive oil should always be extra virgin (EVOO). There is a myth that one should not cook with EVOO, but this is rarely the case. While the smoke point is lower than some other oils, EVOO can be used for most deep frying, the exception being flash frying above 400° F. From sauteeing onions to making salad dressings, a good EVOO will impart much more flavor to your food. Of course, there are very expensive extra virgin olive oils that are incredibly flavorful and best to use as a finishing oil, but most types that you'll find at the grocery store are great for cooking.

BUTTER: I call for unsalted butter in most recipes, which allows salt to be more easily controlled. I tend to reach for European-style butters, which have a higher butterfat content, but that's not a hard and fast rule.

VINEGAR: I use five main types of vinegar in heavy rotation - sherry, apple cider, balsamic, red wine and rice vinegar. In a few recipes I call for balsamic syrup or reduced balsamic. This is to mimic the viscous and slightly sweet flavor of an aged balsamic. Grocery stores sell bottled balsamic syrups, but you can also make your own at a fraction of the cost by reducing regular balsamic vinegar on your stovetop until it becomes the consistency of runny honey. (More on page **41**).

FLOUR: A basic unbleached all-purpose flour is a key pantry ingredient. Using a kitchen scale is the most accurate way to measure flour, however, I provide cup measurements, as well. When measuring flour using cups, use a spoon to "fluff it up" a bit while still in the bag or container, then spoon it into your measuring cup, leveling it with the back of a knife. As flour is stored in the bag, it compresses and you can easily end up with more flour than desired. For those weighing, a cup of all-purpose flour is 120 grams in my recipes. Almond flour is used in a few of my baked goods, and comes in varying forms of coarseness. I call for finely ground almond flour or almond meal.

SUGAR & SWEETENERS: In addition to the standard granulated white, light brown, dark brown and powdered sugars, I sometimes use coconut sugar. It is a less refined sugar with a slight caramel flavor. If you prefer, brown sugar can be substituted. Many of my recipes also incorporate honey or maple syrup, and often I use just a small hit of sweet to accentuate other flavors in the dish. Maple syrup should always be pure maple syrup, not imitation.

VANILLA: Pure vanilla extract will give you the best results and flavor. I recommend it over imitation vanilla.

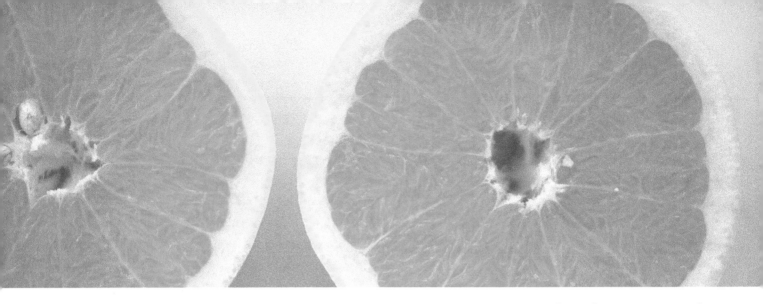

MY ZESTY INGREDIENTS

CITRUS: If you don't enjoy citrus zest, you may want to gift this book to a friend :) I use a lot of zest, it provides so much flavor! And since it is the exterior of the fruit, I always try to buy organic. A few of my recipes call for using a vegetable peeler to get thick strips (which are removed before serving), but most call for using a rasp-style grater, such as Microplane, and measuring the zest in teaspoons. Use only the outermost peel, not the white pith, which can be bitter.

SPICES: A well-stocked spice drawer ensures you can always cook with zest. My short list of "must haves" include allspice, ancho chili powder, cardamom, cinnamon, cumin, garam masala and smoked paprika.

HERBS: Fresh herbs are an invaluable source of flavor in cooking. But, man, those little plastic containers can get expensive! If you can, growing a small herb garden ensures you have what you need on hand. Parsley and cilantro are sold in larger bunches, and to keep these fresh, my method is to wash them in a salad spinner, spin them dry, then store in a large plastic bag with a piece of paper towel. It absorbs extra moisture still present after spinning, and keeps the herbs from wilting. I use this technique for lettuces and leafy greens, as well.

DRIED HERBS: I use tons of dried spices, but not a lot of dried herbs. Dried herbs tend to lose flavor quickly and it's often better to use fresh. A few exceptions are oregano, bay leaf, mint and thyme.

NUTS & SEEDS: Nuts and seeds can go rancid quicker than you think, so if you don't cycle through them often, store them in the freezer. 99% of the time, I call for toasting nuts and seeds before using them to maximize their flavor. My favorite method is to put them on a tray in a toaster oven and toast on the lowest setting, but a dry skillet over medium-low heat also works well. Make sure to shake the skillet often so the nuts or seeds don't scorch, and remove from the heat as soon as they start to take on some color. You will be able to smell the toasted aroma as they are finished.

FRUIT: From berries and citrus, to mangoes and pears, I adore using fruit in savory dishes. Fruit can truly bring the zest, such as in my corn and blackberry salad. A touch of sweet acidity has the ability to completely change the flavor profile in the most delicious way.

CHEESE: A good quality parmigiano is the workhorse of my kitchen; it adds invaluable flavor to so many dishes. Buy a hunk and grate it fresh for the best flavor. Pre-grated cheeses can have an anti-caking agent which affects the natural consistency and moisture content. Gruyere, feta, blue cheese and smoked cheddar are also always in my cheese drawer. I use cheese as flavoring in just about anything. Better cheeses are more expensive, but a little goes a long way in adding flavor, and they store well. A good substitute for gruyere is Comté.

GARLIC & GINGER: My preferred method of using garlic and ginger is to grate them finely on a rasp grater. This saves time over chopping and gives you a finer consistency that blends more evenly into your dishes.

CHILI PEPPERS: Chilis are a very important ingredient in zesty cooking. Fresh chilis such as jalapeño and serrano are easy to find. Thankfully, more and more dried chili varietals are becoming widely available. My recipe for cod stewed with roasted tomatoes calls for guajillo chilis, which are a mild type of dried Mexican chili. If your grocery store doesn't carry them, look for dried ancho chilis instead. A Latin foods market will carry a wide variety of chilis and you should be able to find anything you need there. The process for using dried chilis is simple. Toast them in a dry skillet over medium-low heat until softened, then let them soak in warm water for 10-20 minutes. Discard the stems and seeds before using. Canned chipotle chilis are another invaluable zesty ingredient. They pack a lot of heat, and usually you will only need to use one or two. Transfer the remaining to a small glass jar and they will stay good for a month in your refrigerator.

HARISSA: A jarred pepper-based condiment, harissa comes in both mild and spicy heat levels, and is an easy way to add zest to your cooking. I use it in my lamb quesadillas as well as the eggplant sandwich. It's also wonderful tossed with simple roasted or grilled vegetables, such as fingerling potatoes or grilled asparagus.

TAHINI: A versatile ingredient, tahini can be used in both sweet and savory applications. Make sure to give it a good stir before using to reincorporate the oil, then store the jar in the refrigerator. Don't be tempted to pour off the oil as the tahini will be pasty and dry without it. I prefer Middle Eastern tahini, which is less bitter than Grecian varieties. Try it drizzled over a hot bowl of oatmeal in the morning with a glug of pure maple syrup and sprinkle of cinnamon. Heaven.

FISH SAUCE: Even those who can't stand the smell of fish sauce as an ingredient usually adore the flavor punch it brings to a composed dish. Try it in my Asian shrimp appetizer. The combination of the fish sauce with lime and basil is out of this world.

A NOTE ON ORGANIZATION

This might be the most simple, yet most powerful advice I can offer. Read through the entire recipe two times before getting started. First, when deciding to make a recipe, review the ingredients, ensure you understand the methods and techniques, and check that you have all necessary equipment. Then, before you begin cooking, read through the recipe one more time and plan your approach. I also strongly advise organizing all ingredients just before starting. This is known as *mise-en-place*, "everything in its place". Not only will it streamline your cooking experience, it will help avoid any ingredient hiccups, such as coming to find that an ingredient must be room temperature, not chilled.

IMPORTANT TECHNIQUES

BAKING PRINCIPLES: Baking can be intimidating, but it needn't be. These are my tips for better baking: In **humid climates**, be particularly focused on flour density. Use the fluff, scoop and level method, or better yet, a kitchen scale for accurate measurements. If baking on **convection**, lower oven temp by 25°F. If you are concerned your oven isn't **properly calibrated**, use an oven thermometer; this is a common issue. **Whisk dry ingredients** to ensure they are fully blended, and with an even distribution of leavening agent. **Wet ingredients must be room temperature** for proper cohesion. For example, if melted butter is added to fridge-cold eggs, the butter will solidify, and not properly blend. **At high altitude**, things cook faster. Lower oven temp by 15-25° F and check for doneness earlier than indicated. Also, remove 1 tablespoon of sugar for every 1 cup, and cut leavening (baking soda/powder) by 25%.

BUTTERING PANS: Using a spray is a quick and easy way to ensure your cakes won't stick- but I'm an old fashioned butterer and always will be. In my recipes, I often use parchment paper along with buttering the pan, as it helps the parchment stay in place and line the pan effectively, ensuring your baked goods come out cleanly. In certain recipes, like my zucchini bread, I use parchment as a "sling" to easily lift the loaf from the pan. To do so, simply allow overhang on the long sides to use as handles.

BROWNING BUTTER: Several of my recipes call for brown butter, where butter is melted in a pan on the stove and left to cook until the milk solids turn brown. The moisture content varies greatly in different brands of butter, which will cause more or less foaming and sputtering as it cooks. Typically, the bubbling sound will slow down as it gets close to being done, which can help if there is a lot of foam and it's hard to see the bottom. When in doubt, pour it out into a heat proof bowl and check it, you can always return it to the pan to continue browning but you do not want it to blacken. It can go quickly from brown to black so as soon as it's finished, remove the butter from the pan to stop the cooking process.

ROASTING BELL PEPPERS: Roasted bell peppers come conveniently in jars, however, roasting fresh peppers at home will yield better flavor and texture. Cut the bell peppers into sections along the ribs, removing the stem and seeds. Place on a foil lined baking tray and broil until the skins are blackened. Remove from the oven and wrap the foil around the peppers, allowing them to steam while cooling. This helps to remove the skins. When cool enough to handle, peel, discarding the blackened skin.

BLENDING HOT LIQUIDS: Be very careful when using a blender to puree hot soups or sauces. The heat in the jar will expand, causing the top to pop, and the contents to splatter, which can be dangerous as well as messy. Best bet is to let it cool before blending, or another option is to hold a kitchen towel over the lid of the blender jar VERY firmly as you turn it on to the lowest setting.

USING A DOUBLE BOILER: A simple and protective way of melting an ingredient which can scorch at higher temperatures, such as chocolate, is to use a double boiler. It's also a technique used for making egg white-based frosting or meringue, which you'll find in my semifreddo recipe. If you don't have a double boiler, simply place a metal or pyrex bowl over a pot of simmering water. Importantly, do not let the bottom of the bowl rest in the water, which would heat the contents of the bowl too rapidly.

COOKING GRAINS: Whole grains are a wonderful way to incorporate healthy fiber and nutrients into your diet, while providing dishes with texture and a vehicle for flavor. A common pitfall when cooking grains, such as quinoa, farro, wild rice or barley, is ending up with too much moisture. My technique for dry, fluffy grains is simple and effective. Cook the grains in plenty of water until they are just cooked through (timing varies by grain, check package for specifics). Drain grains using a fine mesh colander, shaking out as much water as you can, then return them to the same pot. Put the lid on and place over low heat for 3-5 minutes. Turn the heat off, then let it rest for another 5-10 minutes with the lid on. Fluff with a fork, and enjoy warm, or let cool for use in salads.

PASTA PERFECTION: The trick to luscious, flavorful pasta lies in a few simple techniques. Use a large pot and generously **salt the cooking water**. Pasta dough rarely includes salt, thus, salting the water seasons it as it cooks. To check if there is enough salt in your water, dip a wooden spoon and after it cools, lick. If the spoon doesn't taste like the ocean, there is not enough salt. **Do not add oil to the cooking water**. It will coat the noodles and not allow your sauce to properly bond. Ensure there is enough room for the pasta to cook; giving the pasta a stir when adding will keep it from sticking. **Cook the pasta only until al dente**, about 1 or 2 minutes shy of being completely done, as it will finish in the accompanying sauce. If you plan to strain your pasta, **scoop a cup or two of the hot, starchy and flavorful cooking water** into a measuring cup. Alternatively, I love using tongs or a large slotted spoon to scoop the pasta directly from the pot into a saucepan, thus, leaving as much of the cooking water as may be needed. If you choose to strain, absolutely **do not rinse your pasta** (only rice noodles may be rinsed). Rinsing the pasta not only cools it off, it removes the starch from the noodles that allows the sauce to bind. **Finish in the saucepan**, tossing pasta with whatever you are serving it with, and as much cooking water is required to keep the pasta loose and from drying out as it finishes cooking. You'd be surprised at how much pasta water you can use! **Taste the pasta before serving**. It may be properly seasoned from its time in the cooking water, however, it could require a pinch more salt, or a grind of black pepper. Finally, **serve it hot!** Pasta waits for no one- it's best served hot, directly from the pan.

SQUEEZE THE DAY: BREAKFAST

I'm one of those people that rises with the sun (or before!), and generally likes a quick breakfast to get my day started. On the weekends, however, we take it easier, and are often more indulgent.

In my breakfast section, you'll find recipes for busy mornings... a comforting apple spiced oatmeal, a do-ahead muesli with fresh mangoes and coconut, and two easy big-batch granolas, as well as brunch fare like custardy overnight french toast, glazed raspberry muffins and a savory asparagus frittata.

A little from column A, a little from column B, as I like to say. All are carefully curated to provide an eye opening, greet the day with a kick in your step kind of meal!

LEMON RASPBERRY MUFFINS

Makes 12 standard size muffins

FOR THE MUFFINS:

10 tablespoons (1 ¼ sticks) unsalted butter, plus more for buttering the pan

1 cup (200 grams) sugar

1 teaspoon pure vanilla extract

1 teaspoon lemon zest

3 large eggs, at room temperature

1 cup (100 grams) almond flour

¾ cup (100 grams) all-purpose flour

¼ teaspoon kosher salt

1 teaspoon baking powder

1 generous cup frozen raspberries (if you buy fresh, freeze them for the recipe)

FOR THE GLAZE:

½ cup powdered sugar

1 tablespoon lemon juice

It might come as a surprise that almond flour is my star ingredient in these muffins, especially given that this recipe calls for lemon zest! When coupled with all-purpose flour, almond flour provides for incredibly moist baked goods with a tender crumb. Pairing these two ingredients is one of my favorite baking methods; here, the combo yields a petite, rich cake (not to be confused with a fluffy, muffin-top muffin). Lemon zest plays an important role, creating a bright and sunny treat - and together with the tart raspberries, is a delightful counterpoint to the glaze, which pushes these into the "dessert for breakfast" realm.

1. Preheat your oven to 350 F. Butter the cavities of a standard muffin pan, or use paper liners.

2. Melt the butter in a small pan, and let it cook over medium heat until the milk solids turn brown. It will bubble and pop while it's cooking, but the sound will start to subside as it becomes close to browning. Stir gently with a silicone spatula, and remove from the heat as soon as you see the butter starting to brown. It can burn very quickly. Transfer to a large bowl, stir in the sugar and set aside to cool for a few minutes. Stir it occasionally to release some of the heat so that it is not too hot when you add the eggs later.

3. Whisk together the all-purpose flour, almond flour, baking powder and salt in a medium bowl.

4. Add the eggs one at a time to the butter mixture, whisking well after each addition. Add the vanilla and lemon zest, then fold in the flour mixture using a silicone spatula. Gently fold in the frozen raspberries. *Freezing the raspberries keeps them from falling apart when you mix them into the batter.*

5. Fill the muffin cavities about ¾ of the way full. I like to use an ice cream / cookie scoop for this, but you can use spoons or a measuring cup if you don't have one. The batter will be quite thin, almost pourable. Bake for 25-30 minutes, until the muffins feel springy to the touch. Remove to a cooling rack.

6. Combine the powdered sugar with the lemon juice so that it is a spreadable consistency. Add more lemon juice if it is too thick, then spread it over the tops of the muffins.

Muffins keep at room temperature for a day, or 2-3 days in the refrigerator.

CHOCOLATE-CHOCOLATE BREAKFAST BREAD

Makes 1 loaf

8 tablespoons (1 stick) unsalted butter, melted, plus more for buttering the pan

¾ cup plus 2 tablespoons (180 gr) dark brown sugar, packed

2 large eggs, at room temperature

¾ cup plain yogurt or sour cream

1 teaspoon pure vanilla extract

1 cup (120 grams) all-purpose flour

½ cup (65 grams) whole wheat flour, or use ½ cup more all-purpose

½ cup (50 grams) cocoa powder

¾ teaspoon ground cinnamon

¾ teaspoon baking soda

½ teaspoon baking powder

¼ teaspoon kosher salt

1 ½ cups (225 grams or ½ pound) zucchini, shredded on the small holes of a box grater

½ cup bittersweet or semisweet chocolate chips

Baking with zucchini is an excellent way to put this prolific veggie to work, adding moistness and texture to cakes, breads and muffins, with minimal effort. It also brings a healthful component, adding fiber and vitamins to this otherwise decadent breakfast treat. And what a treat this is! A rich, chocolate cake, studded with chocolate chips, this bread is also wonderful alongside a cup of tea in the afternoon. I call for using the small holes on a box grater to shred the zucchini, which allows it to melt into the cake without being stringy. You'll find this less sweet than a slice you might find at a typical coffee shop, and we prefer it that way for breakfast.

1. Preheat your oven to 350 F. Butter an 8 x 4-inch loaf pan and line bottom and the long sides with parchment paper. It should create a sort of sling, making it easy to remove the cake after it's baked.

2. Pour the melted butter into a large bowl and then stir in the brown sugar. Whisk in the eggs one at a time and then add the vanilla.

3. Whisk together the flours, cocoa powder, cinnamon, baking soda, baking powder and salt in a medium bowl so that all the dry ingredients are evenly distributed. Stir half into the butter mixture, then mix in the yogurt. The batter will be very thick at this point. Switch to a spatula and stir in the remaining flour. Don't be surprised at how thick the batter is, the zucchini will hydrate it. If you need to, you can use a stand mixer to bring it all together.

4. Stir the zucchini and chocolate chips into the batter, then dump it into the prepared pan. Bake for 50-60 minutes, until the cake feels springy to the touch and has slightly pulled away from the sides. Let it cool in the pan for 10 minutes before turning out onto a rack to cool completely.

Cake can be made ahead of time, wrapped well and kept at room temperature for 2-3 days. It can be frozen for up to a month.

MAPLE CASHEW GRANOLA

3 cups (300 grams) rolled oats, not instant

1 cup raw unsalted cashews

½ cup hemp seed

¼ cup raw unsalted sunflower seeds

2 tablespoons light brown sugar

1 teaspoon ground cinnamon

½ teaspoon ground nutmeg

½ teaspoon kosher salt

⅓ cup coconut oil

6 tablespoons pure maple syrup

1 teaspoon pure vanilla extract

I've been making this granola for more than 15 years - and for good reason. It's simple, flavorful and uses ingredients that I typically have in the pantry. One of those ingredients is coconut oil, which when used in this granola, results in the most perfect crispness. Considered to be a healthier fat than other vegetable oils, it adds a very subtle coconut note. You might not even be able to detect it, yet its nuttiness plays nicely with the cashews, hemp and sunflower seeds. I find myself making double batches to keep up with the demand! Cupfulls get scooped atop creamy yogurt or doused with milk and topped with berries for breakfast in our house - or bagged and tucked into backpacks for snacks. It's a great and healthy addition to the day. If you enjoy dried fruit in your granola, by all means mix in a handful of chopped dried apricots, dried cranberries or golden raisins.

1. Preheat your oven to 275 F. Line a baking sheet with parchment paper.

2. Combine the oats, cashews, hemp seeds, sunflower seeds, salt, brown sugar and spices in a large bowl.

3. Melt the coconut oil with the maple syrup over low heat in a small saucepan. Stir in the vanilla, then pour over the oats and mix thoroughly so that all the ingredients are moistened. Distribute the mixture evenly on the baking sheet and place in the oven. Bake for 45-50 minutes, stirring every 15 minutes.

4. Remove to a rack and let the granola cool completely.

Store in an airtight container for up to two weeks.

GINGERBREAD GRANOLA

3 cups (300 grams) rolled oats, not instant

½ cup ground flax seed (also called flax meal)

⅓ cup (67 grams) dark brown sugar, packed

2 teaspoons ground ginger

2 teaspoon ground cinnamon

¾ teaspoon kosher salt

¼ teaspoon ground cloves

6 tablespoons unsalted butter

3 tablespoons molasses, not blackstrap

2 tablespoons pure maple syrup

1 cup raw unsalted pecans, roughly chopped

⅓ cup chopped crystallized ginger

In the fall and early winter, the scent of gingerbread seems to perpetually waft through our house. From waffles to cakes to oatmeal, there's something about the deep, dark, spiced flavor of gingerbread that is so seasonally comforting. This granola is a sure way to get your fix! Sprinkle it on yogurt, splash it with milk, use it as a crumble topping for baked apples or pears, or simply snack away! But be warned... the crunch is totally addictive! Ginger lovers will adore the chewy sweet crystallized ginger chunks that make this granola next level.

1. Preheat your oven to 250 F. Line a baking sheet with parchment paper.

2. Combine the oats, flax, brown sugar, ground ginger, cinnamon, salt and cloves in a large bowl and stir well.

3. Melt the butter in a small pan with the molasses and maple syrup, stirring to combine. Pour over the oat mixture and stir until all the ingredients are moistened. Turn out onto the prepared baking sheet and place in the oven.

4. Bake the granola, stirring every 10 minutes, for 40-50 minutes. It is dark to begin with, so could be difficult to tell exactly when it is done. Most of the moistness should be gone, and it should be toasted but not burnt.

5. The last 10 minutes of baking, stir in the pecans.

6. Remove to a rack and let the granola cool on the pan. Once cool, add the chopped candied ginger.

Store in an airtight container for up to two weeks.

SPICED APPLE BUTTER OATMEAL WITH PECANS

Serves 2

1 cup (100 grams) rolled oats

2 ¼ cups water

½ teaspoon ground cinnamon

¼ teaspoon ground nutmeg

⅛ teaspoon ground allspice

¼ teaspoon kosher salt

3 tablespoons apple butter

FOR SERVING:

Pure maple syrup

2 tablespoons toasted pecans chopped coarsely

1 tablespoon butter, or a drizzle of milk or cream

When cool weather sets in, there's nothing quite like tucking into a warm bowlful of oatmeal for breakfast. But let's face it, oatmeal requires a flavorful dance partner. Swirling in a few spoonfuls of apple butter and a handful of chopped pecans for crunch, knocks this bowl out of the park - a healthful, tasteful and perfectly fall start to your day. Everyone's got their own favorite way to top oatmeal, and to me it's a big pat of melting butter. If that's not your thing, use milk or cream, or non-dairy milk. The oats definitely benefit from a touch of richness.

1. Combine all the ingredients up to and including the apple butter in a small pot. Bring to a simmer and cook stirring occasionally, for 5-8 minutes until thickened. Divide between two bowls and top with pecans, butter (or milk or cream), and a drizzle of maple syrup.

Note: Apple butter is a product found near jams and jellies, and while its popularity soars in the fall, it is often available year round in many grocery stores. Apple butter contains no butter. It is a thick, spreadable condiment made by slowly cooking apples and cider together until the sugars caramelize, resulting in a rich brown hue.

MANGO MACADAMIA MUESLI

Serves 2

1 cup (100 grams) rolled oats

1 cup plain, unsweetened kefir

2 tablespoons water

¼ teaspoon ground cardamom

⅛ teaspoon ground ginger

¼ teaspoon kosher salt

2 tablespoons honey

½ cup cubed mango, fresh or frozen

2 tablespoons macadamia nuts (about 8 nuts), coarsely chopped

2 tablespoons flaked toasted coconut, not shredded

Loaded with fresh summer fruit, and cool, creamy kefir, muesli is an easy, healthful and tasty way to start the day. You might know muesli as "overnight oats," but if it's not something you are familiar with, this is a fun introduction. Fresh mangoes, chopped macadamia nuts and crunchy, toasted coconut lend a tropical vibe, but what makes the recipe really special is the cardamom. Cardamom's flavor is difficult to describe, giving this dish that "je ne sais quoi" appeal. It is very aromatic and a tad fruity, an excellent companion for the mango. A note on using cardamom: It packs a powerful punch. The muesli will be balanced if you add the correct proportion of toppings. If you choose to not use the macadamia nuts or coconut, decrease the cardamom by half. Portion into small mason jars for easy grab-and-go breakfasts, triple the recipe to feed a crowd.

Note: Kefir is a milk product that is similar to yogurt, though thinner and pourable. It is found in the dairy section of grocery stores, and is often flavored or sweetened. For this recipe use plain, unsweetened kefir. As a substitute you may use plain, whole milk yogurt (not Greek), but will need to add a tablespoon or more of water to thin to the right consistency and make pourable.

1. In a small bowl, combine all the ingredients except the nuts and coconut, and mix well. Refrigerate overnight. Before serving, sprinkle with the nuts and coconut flakes. *If you will not be using the toppings, decrease the cardamom to ⅛ teaspoon.*

Muesli will keep for 4-5 days refrigerated.

OVERNIGHT FRENCH TOAST WITH PEAR MAPLE SYRUP

Generously Serves 5

FOR THE FRENCH TOAST:

14 ounce loaf brioche, or other soft egg bread, sliced ¾" thick (approx. 10 slices)

3 tablespoons very soft butter, unsalted

4 large eggs

2 cups whole milk

¼ cup heavy cream

¼ cup sugar

¼ teaspoon kosher salt

½ teaspoon ground cinnamon

¼ teaspoon ground cardamom

1 teaspoon pure vanilla extract

⅓ cup walnuts, very coarsely chopped, optional

FOR THE PEAR SYRUP:

½ cup pear preserves

¼ cup maple syrup

Note: If you have trouble finding pear preserves, you can make your own at home by simmering 1 peeled and diced pear with ¼ cup water and 2-3 tablespoons of sugar until very thick and soft, about 30 minutes. If you have a very ripe, sweet pear, use less sugar.

This dish falls firmly in the "dessert for breakfast" category. Unabashedly, this is a special morning treat - but what makes it even MORE special is that it's prepared the night before so whomever first awakens need only pop the baker in the oven to fill the house with an incredible, bakery-like aroma. The icing on the cake, as they say, is a luscious, pear syrup for drizzling. Special occasions call for a decadent breakfast bake. What are you waiting for?

1. Butter each side of each slice of bread with a very thin layer of butter. It's important that the butter is room temperature so that it doesn't tear the bread. Lay the slices slightly overlapping in a buttered baking dish. They should be tight together and mostly flat so that they can absorb the liquid as they sit overnight. You can cut them in half diagonally (as I have in the photo) so that they fit a smaller 7 x 9-inch dish, or leave the slices whole and use a larger 9 x 12-inch baking dish.

2. Whisk together the eggs, milk, cream, sugar, salt, cinnamon, cardamom and vanilla in a medium bowl. Pour over the bread evenly, cover with foil and refrigerate overnight.

3. In the morning, preheat your oven to 350 F. Place the baking dish in the oven, covered, and bake for 20 minutes. Turn the heat down to 325 F, remove the foil and, if using, scatter the walnuts evenly over the top. Bake for another 15 minutes until puffed and golden. When pressed on lightly, there should be no liquid coming up from the bread.

4. While the french toast is baking, make the syrup by warming the preserves and the maple syrup over low heat. Stir so that they are evenly combined.

5. To serve, scoop a slice of the french toast onto plates and drizzle with the pear syrup.

SAVORY GRAIN BOWL WITH CRISPY EGG & AVOCADO

Serves 2

½ cup hulled or pearled barley

¾ teaspoon kosher salt, divided use

1 ½ tablespoons butter

4 ounces sliced cremini mushrooms or mini portobellos

½ teaspoon ancho chili powder

2 large eggs

½ large ripe avocado, pitted and sliced

Chili oil or hot sauce for serving

Note: There are two types of barley, pearled and hulled. I call for hulled barley as it retains more nutrients than pearled barley. Because it still has its bran layer intact, the grains cook up less starchy and less glutinous, and will be more fluffy and separated. If you're short on time, you can use pearled barley, which cooks twice as quickly (approx. 20-25 minutes). Think of it as the difference between white and brown rice.

This hearty, healthy breakfast bowl will keep you fueled until lunch. Fiber rich grains are topped with creamy avocado, protein packed egg, and my favorite, mushrooms sauteed with zesty ancho chili powder. It's a symphony of textures and flavors. Drizzle the finished dish with a spicy chili oil or splash with your favorite hot sauce. If you prefer to go light on the heat, a mild salsa will be nice.

1. Cook the barley with salt in plenty of water until tender (about 40 minutes for hulled barley, 20 minutes for pearled). Drain and return to the pot, cover with a lid, and place back over very low heat for 2-3 minutes to steam the remaining moisture from the grains. Turn it off and keep it covered to stay warm while you cook the mushrooms and eggs.

2. Melt 1 tablespoon of the butter in a medium skillet. When it's hot, add the mushrooms, ancho chili powder, and ½ teaspoon salt. Cook until softened, 4-5 minutes. Remove the mushrooms from the pan, then add the remaining ½ tablespoon butter and place back over medium-high heat. Crack the eggs into the pan, careful to not break the yolks, and immediately turn the heat to low. Sprinkle each egg with a pinch of salt. If you like your yolks runny, flip gently and cook just until the whites are set. If you like them more well cooked, flip the eggs over and cook for 2 minutes on the other side.

3. Divide the barely into two bowls. Add equal amounts of mushroom and avocado to each bowl, and top them with the eggs. Serve with your favorite hot sauce or chili oil.

Fry your perfect egg:

Sunny side up   The yolk is face up, not flipped, and is cooked only until the white is set but yolk remains runny.

Over easy   Similar to sunny side up, however, the egg is carefully flipped before the white is fully set. This is my preferred method as you can cook the white more quickly and still keep a slightly runny yolk.

Over medium   Similar to over easy, however, the yolk is cooked to a custardy consistency.

Over well/hard   The egg is turned and the yolk is fully cooked through.

CHEESY BAKED ASPARAGUS FRITTATA TOPPED WITH PROSCIUTTO

Serves 6

1 tablespoon unsalted butter, plus more for buttering the dish

1 small shallot, finely chopped

3 sprigs fresh thyme, leaves stripped from the stems

½ pound thin asparagus, trimmed, cut into ½" lengths

2 tablespoons white wine, or use water or broth

8 large eggs

4 ounces gruyere, grated on the large holes of a box grater

½ teaspoon kosher salt

5 thin slices of prosciutto

Freshly cracked black pepper

Note: When shopping for asparagus, 1 bunch, once the tough bottom stalks are trimmed off, usually yields about ½ pound.

Frittatas are a wonderfully simple, yet versatile, brunch dish, easily straddling the middle ground between AM and PM. I also frequently serve frittatas for dinner on busy weeknights, as they come together quickly, and can be made to include whatever I have on hand. Asparagus, gruyere and prosciutto make happy friends- and a vibrant breakfast bite. Gruyere brings an unmistakable flavor punch, and earns the starring role in this dish. Leftovers can be tucked into a warm ciabatta bun, with a little tomato jam or sweet onion jam, for a great sandwich.

1. Preheat your oven to 375 F. Butter a deep 9-inch ceramic pie plate and set aside.

2. Melt the butter in a small skillet and cook the shallots with a pinch of salt until softened, about 3 minutes. Add the asparagus and thyme, cooking for 1-2 minutes until just slightly tender. Turn the heat up to high and add the splash of wine or water and cook until the asparagus are softened and the liquid has evaporated. Remove from the heat and transfer to the prepared baking dish.

3. Whisk the eggs and salt together in a medium bowl, then stir in the gruyere and plenty of freshly cracked black pepper. Pour the eggs on top of the asparagus in the prepared pan, then lay the slices of prosciutto on top, crumpling them a little as they nestle into the eggs.

4. Place the dish in the oven and bake for 25-30 minutes, or until it is golden brown and springy to the touch. Cut into wedges to serve warm or room temperature.

BREAKFAST TACOS WITH A KICK

Serves 4

FOR THE SALSA:

1 cup canned or cooked black beans, rinsed and drained

1 small Mandarin orange, such as a "Cutie" or satsuma, each segment cut into 2 or 3 pieces

½ small white onion, chopped, about ⅓ cup

¼ cup cilantro, chopped

Juice of ½ lime

1 tablespoon honey

½ teaspoon ground cumin

½ teaspoon kosher salt

1 teaspoon adobo sauce from the can of chipotle chilis

FOR THE TACOS:

1 tablespoon unsalted butter

6 large eggs

1 chipotle chili from a can, seeded and chopped

½ teaspoon kosher salt

1 cup shredded mild white cheese, such as Monterrey Jack

8 corn tortillas, Mi Rancho® brand preferred

These are not just one of my favorite *breakfast* tacos, they are one of my *all time* favorite tacos! (And that's saying a lot given my love of stuff stuffed in tortillas). Chipotle chilis bring the kick and deliver a smoky sweetness that goes so well with the orange salsa. The eggs bring them into the breakfast realm, but they can be enjoyed any time of day.

1. Prepare the salsa by adding all of the ingredients to a bowl and combining well. Now move on to making the tacos.

2. Warm the butter in a large non-stick or ceramic skillet. Whisk together the eggs, salt and chopped chipotle chili in a medium bowl, then add to the hot pan. Cook the scrambled eggs in the pan until just cooked through - use a heat proof spatula to gently turn them while cooking to create large curds. Turn off the heat but keep in the pan so they stay warm.

3. Heat a griddle or large dry skillet. Cook the tortillas about 1 minute per side over medium heat. When they are heated through, top each one with an equal amount of cheese and turn heat to low. Cook until the cheese just begins to melt. *If your cooking surface isn't large enough to make all 8 at once, do them in batches.*

4. To serve, place two tortillas on each plate. Top with equal amounts of the scrambled eggs, then spoon the salsa over top. Pass any extra salsa at the table.

SALADS, SOUPS & SANDWICHES

While these dishes frequently appear on my table in the afternoon, they are also in regular rotation for dinner. Salads are often overlooked and underappreciated... this is unfortunate! When done well, salads can be the highlight of a meal, and can be tossed together without much fuss. Secrets to a good salad lie primarily in the art of balancing and layering flavors, and most importantly, in making your own dressing.

These principals hold true for soups and sandwiches, as well! Layering of flavors - quite literally in sandwiches - including a contrast of textures and flavors, and a bit of zest to make it all pop, are your keys to success!

Several of my salads call for reduced balsamic, which is also known as balsamic syrup or balsamic glaze. These can be purchased in the vinegar section of most grocery stores, or you can easily make your own by cooking down regular balsamic vinegar at a simmer until it is reduced by about half. When purchased, balsamic syrups oftentimes come flavored. For my recipes, an unflavored version is best.

If you can find an ingredient called saba, which is a cooked grape must condiment, it tastes more like a refined aged balsamic than most syrups do, but it is on the pricey side and usually is only sold at specialty stores. I have one recipe that calls for saba, but using balsamic syrup instead is a good substitution.

BEET, AVOCADO & KALE SALAD WITH PICKLED PEACHES AND ORANGE BALSAMIC VINAIGRETTE

Serves 4

FOR THE SALAD:

2 medium beets, red or yellow, trimmed and scrubbed

2 packed cups curly leaf kale, washed and chopped

1 ripe avocado, cubed

¼ cup fresh basil, torn into pieces if the leaves are large

¼ cup Marcona almonds

FOR THE PICKLED PEACHES:

1 firm peach, cut into wedges about ½" thick, or use frozen peaches

1 tablespoon honey

½ cup apple cider vinegar

A pinch of salt

FOR THE DRESSING:

1 tablespoon fresh orange juice

1 tablespoon fresh lemon juice

1 small garlic clove, grated, about ½ teaspoon

1 tablespoon reduced balsamic vinegar or purchased balsamic syrup

¾ teaspoon kosher salt

1 teaspoon honey

½ teaspoon ground sumac, optional

3 tablespoons extra virgin olive oil

One summer day I brought home a basket of pretty looking peaches and set them on the counter. And waited, and waited, and waited. Days later, they were still rock hard. I cut one open and it had started to discolor in the middle, but not ripen. Huh. Still edible, but totally subpar as a fresh peach, I thought, pickle it! I sliced it up, tossed it in a jar, and covered it with cider vinegar. Turns out, they were great on everything from salad, to salsas, and on sandwiches. Pickled peaches bring the zest in this recipe! The crunchy almonds, fragrant basil, and creamy avocado are the cherry on top. You don't need subpar peaches to make this of course! But they should be on the firm side, not totally ripe yet. Frozen peaches can be substituted when not in season.

1. Begin by roasting your beets. Preheat the oven to 350 F. Scrub the beets clean with a vegetable brush, trim off the stems and root if it is long, then wrap in foil. Place on a baking dish or sheet pan and roast for an hour. If your beets are on the smaller side, they will take less time. Remove from the oven and let cool completely. Once cool, slip off the skins and cut into cubes. This can be done a day in advance.

2. Make the pickled peaches while the beets roast. Place the peach wedges in a clean jar. Mix together the cider vinegar, honey and a pinch of salt and pour over the peaches. Let sit at room temperature for at least an hour before using, and up to a week in the refrigerator.

3. Place all of the ingredients for the salad in a bowl (kale, almonds, cubed avocado, torn basil, cooled and cut beets). Remove about half of the peaches from their liquid and cut into a large dice. Add to the salad bowl. You can prep all of this ahead of time and refrigerate, undressed, until ready to serve. The avocado can begin to turn brown if cut too far in advance, so if you are preparing the salad ahead of time, don't cut the avocado until ready to toss together.

4. Whisk all of the ingredients for the dressing together. This can also be done ahead and refrigerated. When ready to serve the salad, toss together with the dressing. The kale will become softer the longer it sits, so if you prefer your kale salads this way, let it sit about 15 minutes before serving.

You will only use half of the pickled peach for the salad. If you prefer not to have any left over, halve the amounts (and eat the other half of the peach :)

SUMMERTIME PLUM, TOMATO & BLUE CHEESE CAPRESE

Serves 4

1 pound ripe summer tomatoes (about 2 large), preferably heirloom

2 ripe red plums

8-10 large basil leaves

4 ounces Stilton, crumbled, or similar blue cheese

2 tablespoons extra virgin olive oil

2 tablespoons saba, or use a thick balsamic syrup, sometimes also called a balsamic glaze

2 teaspoons flaked sea salt, such as Maldon

Note: I recommend a Stilton for this salad, not only because it is one of the best, but also due to its relative dryness and ability to crumble. If you cannot find Stilton, use a similar dry blue cheese. Stay away from creamy gorgonzola or pungent Roquefort for this application.

Caprese salads are named for the small island off the coast of Italy where the famed tomato, basil, mozzarella trio was born. Today, the term has evolved to broadly describe composed salads which highlight fresh produce, cheese and herbs. My spin uses fresh plums and crumbly, blue cheese, along with perfectly juicy tomatoes, topped with a simple drizzle of olive oil and a cooked grape must condiment, called saba. Saba is generally found at specialty grocers, and is similar in flavor and consistency to a refined aged balsamic. If you cannot locate saba, substitute aged balsamic or balsamic syrup, which will do the trick.

1. Slice the tomatoes and the plums and place them, overlapping, in a large, shallow bowl or wide platter. Tear the basil leaves and crumble the Stilton and sprinkle both over top.

2. When ready to serve, drizzle with the oil and vinegar, and sprinkle with the sea salt.

ROMAINE WITH CORN, BLACKBERRIES, MANCHEGO & PUMPKIN SEEDS

Serves 4

FOR THE VINAIGRETTE:

1 tablespoon finely chopped shallot

1 teaspoon fresh rosemary, chopped

2 tablespoons lime juice

1 tablespoon red wine vinegar

2 teaspoons honey

½ teaspoon ground cumin

½ teaspoon smoked paprika

1 teaspoon kosher salt

Freshly ground black pepper

¼ cup extra virgin olive oil

FOR THE SALAD:

1 head romaine lettuce, washed and spun dry

¾ cup cooked corn kernels

½ heaping cup blackberries, halved if large

2 tablespoons hulled pumpkin seeds, lightly toasted

½ cup aged Manchego cheese, grated on the large holes of a box grater

My guiding principles for composing a well-balanced salad: Use something sweet, something salty, fatty, and acidic, incorporate something crunchy and include fresh herbs. This green salad ticks all the boxes. Sweet tender corn and summer blackberries are a true match made in heaven, and are set off by the rich manchego cheese, crunchy pumpkin seeds, crisp lettuce and tart lime juice in the dressing. What truly makes this successful, though, is the zippy shallot vinaigrette. The lime juice and red wine vinegar mellow the sharpness of the shallot, leaving a sweet onion essence that is bolstered by the smoked paprika and ground cumin. A touch of honey smooths it all out.

1. Whisk all of the ingredients for the salad dressing together, or place in a jar with a tight fitting lid and shake vigorously. I like to do the latter so that I can make it ahead of time and keep it in the fridge until serving. Sometimes the honey gets stuck to the bottom - if this happens just give it a stir with a fork or a small whisk to incorporate it.

2. Place all of the salad ingredients in a bowl. This can also be done ahead of time (undressed), covered and refrigerated. When ready to serve, toss the salad with the dressing. Use your judgment on how much dressing to use. Depending on the size of your head of lettuce, you may not need all of it.

HARICOTS VERTS IN FIG JAM VINAIGRETTE WITH SHAVED PARMIGIANO, HAZELNUTS & CRISPY PROSCIUTTO

Serves 4

FOR THE VINAIGRETTE:

2 tablespoons fig jam

1 tablespoon balsamic vinegar

½ teaspoon garlic powder

¾ teaspoon kosher salt

½ teaspoon honey

1 tablespoon fresh lemon juice

2 tablespoons extra virgin olive oil, plus a little extra for cooking the prosciutto

FOR THE SALAD:

¾ pound haricot verts, french style very thin green beans, trimmed

Hunk of parmigiano reggiano (you will not use all)

4 slices of prosciutto, about 1 ounce

2 tablespoon hazelnuts, toasted, skins rubbed off and roughly chopped

Freshly cracked black pepper

There was a spell when my kids were obsessed with a certain cooking show on television, where contestants receive mystery baskets, and create their own dishes combining some pretty unique stuff. One of my kids sent in a video and photos of her creations, and applied to be on the show. To practice, I'd give her mystery ingredients and she would decide what to make. This fig vinaigrette was born one of those nights. I never would have thought to use fig jam to make this supremely satisfying and delightful salad dressing, but thank goodness that she did! It's amazing on any number of salads, especially those with salty counterpoints to tame its sweetness. Here, savory prosciutto and parmigiano fit the bill. So how did it turn out with the application? My daughter received a call to go to New York to audition! Alas, life got in the way, and sadly we couldn't make the trip, so she never did get her shot... the consolation prize for us was this fabulous recipe!

1. Begin by making the vinaigrette. Place the fig jam and balsamic in a small saucepan over medium heat. After it starts to bubble around the edges, turn the heat to low and let it cook until reduced slightly and thickened, about 2 minutes. Remove from the heat and add the garlic powder, salt, honey and olive oil. Set aside to cool. Once it is mostly cooled (still a little warm is fine, but not hot), stir in the lemon juice. The mixture will be quite thick, but should emulsify if you give it a good stir with a small whisk or fork.

2. Next, make the crispy prosciutto. Pour a layer of olive oil in a medium skillet, about a tablespoon or more if you need it, to cover the bottom. Warm over medium heat, then add the prosciutto in one layer. Cook for 1-2 minutes, then flip it over. It should crisp up and shrink a little. Remove to a paper towel lined plate. Repeat with any slices that didn't fit in the first round. Once cool, break or chop into bite sized pieces. Pour any extra oil from the pan into the fig jam dressing - it has great flavor!

3. Steam the green beans until soft, which should take roughly 8 minutes. You could also boil them in salted water if you don't have a steamer basket, and drain them well. They should be thoroughly cooked, but still retain a little bite. Place the cooked beans in a serving bowl and toss with the fig jam vinaigrette.

4. Using a vegetable peeler, shave 20 thick strips of cheese on top of the beans, then top with the pieces of prosciutto and chopped nuts. Toss at the table.

You can make the dressing and cook the beans ahead of time and keep them refrigerated. Do not toss the beans with the dressing until just before serving, as they will lose their vibrant color.

ROASTED CHERRY TOMATO & BUTTERNUT SQUASH SALAD WITH LIME VINAIGRETTE

In early fall I can be found scattering this butternut/tomato combo atop pizza - one of my faves. One night I was craving the flavors, but hadn't made any dough. Hmm, why not turn it into a salad? In a word, yum! Acidity from the dressing brought out the vegetable's sweetness, and I didn't even miss the crust. The highlight of the dish is the ginger roasted cherry tomatoes. Cooking the fruit concentrates their flavor, and they become jammy and sweet, a perfect complement to the maple roasted squash. Mozzarella lends a creaminess and mellows the spice; cashews add the crunch. Plan a bit ahead for this dish, as the squash and tomatoes need to cool before assembling the salad so as to not wilt the spinach.

Serves 4

FOR THE VINAIGRETTE:

½ lime, zest plus 1 tablespoon juice

1 tablespoon rice vinegar

1 teaspoon mirin

1 small garlic clove (about ½ teaspoon), grated or crushed

½ teaspoon kosher salt

1 ½ tablespoons extra virgin olive oil

Note: Mirin is a Japanese rice wine found on the shelves near soy sauce, rice vinegars and other Asian ingredients.

FOR THE SALAD:

2 tablespoons plus 1 teaspoon extra virgin olive oil

1 small butternut squash (about a 2 pound squash) peeled, seeded, and cut into ½" cubes

1 tablespoon chopped rosemary

2 teaspoons kosher salt

1 ½ tablespoons pure maple syrup

1 ½ cups multi-colored grape tomatoes, large ones halved

1 teaspoon freshly grated ginger

5 ounces baby spinach

¼ cup unsalted cashews, toasted lightly

4 ounces fresh mozzarella

Freshly cracked black pepper

Red pepper flakes, optional

1. Make the vinaigrette. Combine the zest from the half lime, lime juice, vinegar, mirin, garlic and salt in a small bowl. Whisk, and then pour in the olive oil. *This can be made a few hours ahead and refrigerated.*

2. Preheat your oven to 350 F. Toss the squash with the rosemary, 1 ½ teaspoons of the salt and 2 tablespoons of the olive oil on a roasting pan or large baking dish. In a separate, small baking dish or oven proof skillet, toss the tomatoes with the remaining 1 teaspoon olive oil, ginger and ½ teaspoon salt. Place both vegetables in the oven and roast, stirring occasionally, for 30-35 minutes or until the squash is cooked through. The tomatoes should be nicely roasted with some color, and have released some of their juice into the pan. Remove from the oven, and stir the maple syrup into the squash. Let everything cool.

3. To assemble, place the spinach in the bottom of a large flat salad bowl. Top with the squash and tomatoes. Tear the cheese into pieces and place in the bowl, then scatter the cashews on top. *Salad can be prepared up to this point (undressed) and refrigerated for a few hours. Let it come back to room temperature for optimal flavor.* Just before serving, stir the dressing well and toss with the salad, topping with some freshly cracked black pepper and a sprinkle of red pepper flakes, if desired.

FARRO SALAD WITH CHICKEN, MANDARIN ORANGES, AVOCADO, FETA & PISTACHIOS

Serves 4

FOR THE SALAD:

1 cup farro

2 fresh Mandarin oranges, peeled, segmented and segments cut in half

½ cup crumbled feta

¼ cup shelled pistachios

1 medium avocado, peeled, pitted and cut into cubes

1 medium cooked chicken breast (a heaping cup), cubed

¼ cup fresh mint, chopped

FOR THE VINAIGRETTE:

2 tablespoons fresh lemon juice

1 tablespoon sherry vinegar

½ teaspoon ground cumin

¼ teaspoon allspice

2 teaspoons pure maple syrup

1 teaspoon kosher salt

Freshly cracked black pepper

4 tablespoons extra virgin olive oil

Note: Cuties and satsumas are both varieties of Mandarin oranges and either can be used.

This hearty, grain-based salad's strength is in its portability. Well, that and its incredibly delicious flavor and texture combos. Farro is a type of wheat, which cooks up fluffy and without a lot of starch. Perfect for cold salads, the grains stay separated and not gummy. You'll find oranges add a sweet acidity that so nicely offsets the brininess of feta. Though the stars of the show are pistachios, offering an intense nuttiness and all-important crunch. I often bring this salad to potlucks or on picnics, as it holds up so well during transport. As with any salad, tossing with the vinaigrette at the last minute is key.

1. Begin by cooking the farro. Place the grains in a medium saucepan and cover with water by at least two inches. Stir in ½ teaspoon salt, bring to a simmer and cook until the grains are tender. *The amount of time will depend on the type of farro you buy, so check the package directions.* When fully cooked but not mushy, drain the farro in a mesh strainer and return to the pot. Cover with a lid, return to the stove over low heat, and let it steam for 2 minutes. Turn off the heat and let it sit for 10 minutes, then remove the lid, fluff with a fork and let cool. *You can remove it to a bowl to cool faster if you like, which will also help any remaining moisture evaporate from the grains. The goal is to remove as much moisture as possible, so that the dressing isn't diluted.*

2. To the bowl with the cooled farro, add the feta, oranges, pistachos, avocado and mint. Mix the vinaigrette ingredients in a small bowl or shake vigorously in a jar with a lid, pour over the salad and toss.

The salad can be assembled and refrigerated, undressed, a few hours ahead. Sprinkle with the fresh mint just before serving.

BROTHY TOFU & RICE NOODLE SOUP

Serves 4

1 tablespoon neutral oil or butter

1 small shallot, chopped

4 garlic cloves, chopped

½ teaspoon kosher salt

2 slices peeled ginger, each slice about ⅛" thick

4 cups low-sodium chicken broth

1 large sweet potato, peeled and cut into ½" cubes

8 ounce block firm or extra firm tofu, cut into cubes

4 tablespoons soy sauce

8 teaspoons fish sauce

8 teaspoons coconut sugar or light brown sugar

4 tablespoons lemon juice

1 or 2 serrano chilis, stemmed and split in half, optional

8 ounces rice noodles

Chopped fresh cilantro or torn basil leaves for serving

I debated whether or not to include this soup. Yes, it's totally delicious... but we have it so frequently, it's no longer top of mind as a *special* creation. Everyone loves it, and since I can get it on the table in under 20 minutes, it certainly deserves a spot! An Asian-inspired, brothy, noodle-loaded soup, it doesn't draw from any specific region, combining a few simple ingredients into a flavor packed bowlful of comfort. Freshly squeezed lemon juice, when combined with fish sauce, soy sauce, and coconut sugar, develops into a supremely satisfying broth. If tofu isn't for you, you can substitute cooked chicken or shrimp. I often toss in other veggies that I have in the fridge, like broccoli, mushrooms or peas.

1. Place the oil or butter in a large saucepan or stockpot. Saute the shallot and garlic with ½ teaspoon salt for 2 minutes. Pour in the broth and add the pieces of sliced ginger and sweet potato. Bring to a simmer and cook until the sweet potato is tender, about 12-15 minutes. Add the cubed tofu, turn the heat to low, and cover partially to keep warm.

2. Get out four large, deep soup bowls. To each bowl, add one tablespoon soy sauce, two teaspoons of the fish sauce, and 2 teaspoons of the sugar. Squeeze a scant tablespoon of lemon juice into each bowl, and if you are using the chilis, drop a half chili into each bowl (for whomever wants the heat).

3. Cook the noodles according to package directions. If you aren't familiar with cooking rice noodles, be aware that they can stick together easily and benefit from stirring as soon as they go in the pot, as well as a few times while cooking. Drain and rinse with cool water, which will further help the noodles from sticking. Divide the noodles equally between the four bowls, and stir each bowl to mix; this will help to flavor the noodles before the broth is added. Discard the ginger, and ladle the broth, sweet potato and tofu into each bowl. Stir to distribute the seasoning liquid from the bottom of the bowl throughout the broth.

4. Sprinkle with a little cilantro or basil, if using (I like both!) and serve.

My middle daughter always asks for more fish sauce! So we put the bottle on the table in case anyone wants to add another dash.

MUSHROOM LEEK SOUP WITH CASHEW CREAM

I didn't set out for this to be a vegan soup, but as I started developing and testing the recipe, it kept drawing me in that direction. And you know what? Incorporating miso, and the rich cashew cream swirl on top, yields a depth of flavor and heartiness typically only achieved from bone broth or added cream. Bread acts as a thickener, creating an ideally smooth texture. Be careful when blending hot liquids, as I note in the recipe instructions. I advocate using a blender for the best results, but if you have a very good immersion blender you can try that instead. A note on the cashew cream: You'll need to plan ahead as the cashews soak for a few hours to soften before blending. If you have a very high powered blender, such as a Vitamix, you can cut down on the soaking time to just 30 minutes.

Serves 4

FOR THE SOUP:

3 tablespoons extra virgin olive oil

1 large leek (about 1 cup), tough green stem removed, washed well and chopped

2 large garlic cloves, chopped

¾ teaspoon kosher salt

1 pound cremini mushrooms, washed, trimmed and roughly chopped

8 sage leaves, chopped

Freshly cracked black pepper

½ cup white wine

3 ½ cups vegetable broth

2 tablespoons white miso

1 ½ cups cubed or roughly torn bread, crusts removed

FOR THE CASHEW CREAM:

½ cup raw unsalted cashews

¼ cup water

1 tablespoon olive oil

1 small garlic clove

½ teaspoon kosher salt

1 teaspoon lemon juice or white wine vinegar

1. Begin by making the cashew cream. Soak the nuts in water to cover for 4 hours. Drain, rinse and place in a blender with the remaining ingredients. Puree for 1-2 minutes until very thick and creamy. If your blender is getting stuck, you can add more water, one teaspoon at a time, to help it out. *Cashew cream can be made a day ahead and kept refrigerated.*

2. For the soup, warm the olive oil over medium heat in a large saucepan or stock pot. Add the leeks, garlic and ½ teaspoon of the salt and cook for 5 minutes over medium-low heat until softened. Add the mushrooms, sage and remaining ¼ teaspoon salt and raise the heat to high. Cook for 3 or 4 minutes, stirring often. The mushrooms should give off some of their liquid. Pour in the wine and simmer briskly for a minute before adding 3 cups of the broth. Bring back to a simmer and cook for 10 minutes.

3. Remove from the heat and stir in the miso and bread. Use an immersion blender, or for the creamiest soup, place in a blender and puree. Be very careful when blending hot liquids as the steam can build up in the blender jar and cause the top to pop off and the contents to splatter. If you have time, it is helpful to let the soup cool slightly. Only fill the jar half full, and using a kitchen towel over the blender, keep a very firm hand on the lid while blending the hot soup. Once thoroughly blended (you will probably need to do this in 2 or 3 batches), return the soup to the pot and keep warm over low heat. If it is too thick, add a little more vegetable broth.

4. To serve, ladle into bowls, swirl 1 or 2 tablespoons of the cashew cream into the soup, and top with freshly cracked black pepper.

WHITE BEAN & CELERY ROOT SOUP WITH SAUSAGE

Serves 6

FOR THE SOUP:

2 tablespoons extra virgin olive oil

1 pound sweet Italian style sausage, chicken, turkey or pork

1 small onion, chopped

4 large garlic cloves, chopped

1 medium celery root, peeled and cubed

1 large carrot, diced

½ cup white wine

4 fresh thyme sprigs

4 cups low-sodium chicken broth

½ teaspoon kosher salt

28 ounce can white beans, drained and rinsed

FOR THE CROUTONS:

3 cups cubed sourdough bread

¼ cup extra virgin olive oil

2 large garlic cloves, chopped finely

½ teaspoon kosher salt

Freshly cracked black pepper

I learned this trick years ago from a British friend who "had us round" for lunch one day. She served the most lovely white bean soup, from which she had taken a little out and pureed it, then added it back to the soup. The result was a creamy, *creamless* soup, rich with flavor, but with nothing heavy to weigh us down midday. I use this technique all the time now, to create the consistency everyone loves, without reaching for the carton of cream. The celery root further bolsters the richness and flavor, and the sourdough croutons make for the perfect crunch, elevating it to a special, stand alone meal.

1. Warm the olive oil in a large saucepan or stock pot. Cook the sausage, breaking it up slightly with a spoon. When it is fully cooked, remove to a plate with a slotted spoon. If you are using pork sausage, pour the excess fat out of the skillet, leaving only a generous tablespoon.

2. Add the onions and a pinch of salt to the pot and cook over medium heat until softened, about 8 minutes. Add the garlic, celery root and carrot, and stir while cooking for 1-2 minutes. Pour in the wine and bring to a simmer, letting the wine reduce by half. Add the broth, thyme sprigs and ½ teaspoon salt, bring to a simmer and cook until the celery root is tender, about 10 minutes.

3. Remove from the heat and stir in the beans. Scoop out roughly ⅓ of the soup and place it in a blender. Cover lid with a kitchen towel and be very careful when blending hot liquids as the steam can build up and cause the top to pop off and the contents to splatter. If you prefer, you could use an immersion blender to puree about ⅓ of the soup directly in the pot. If using the blender, return the pureed soup to the pot and add the sausage back in. Taste for seasoning and add more salt, if needed. Partially cover and keep warm over low heat.

4. Meanwhile, make the croutons. Warm the oil over medium heat in a large skillet. Add the bread and cook, stirring, until it starts to turn golden brown. Once it has toasted evenly, turn the heat to low and add the garlic and salt. Cook for a minute, stirring, then remove from the heat.

5. To serve, remove the thyme sprigs, and ladle the soup into bowls. Divide the croutons among the bowls, top with freshly cracked black pepper and serve warm.

SANDWICHES FROM AROUND THE WORLD

I studied in the Loire valley, southwest of Paris, France. I have a LOT of food memories from my time in Tours, but funny enough, some of the most memorable do not involve French cuisine. There was one "rue" we'd stroll down, with an array of international cafés selling the most amazing street food. A Vietnamese shop with fresh spring rolls that would blow your mind; a Middle Eastern döner kebab joint with its tender meat slowly rotating on the vertical spit; and a hole in the wall Italian panini place that used goat cheese from a local fromagerie, spread on the most ethereal bread. I loved that each took advantage of the beautiful local ingredients, incorporating them into their traditional foods. Their creations were the ultimate representation of time and place.

That's a bit how we all must cook when we branch out into international cuisines. We may not have galangal root or fresh curry leaves. We improvise with what we have, creating dishes that are the definition of "fusion" cooking.

These sandwiches are inspired from some of my favorite classic sandwiches from around the world, but with my own spin and perspective that brings them home. There's no limit to the yummy stuff you can put between bread!

GARLICKY KALE PANINI WITH SWEET TOMATO JAM, GRUYERE & PANCETTA

Serves 4

FOR THE TOMATO JAM:

14 ounce can diced tomatoes

⅓ cup sugar

¼ teaspoon cumin

¾ teaspoon freshly grated ginger

½ teaspoon smoked paprika

A pinch of kosher salt

FOR THE KALE:

1 tablespoon extra virgin olive oil

4 ounces pancetta, diced

1 bunch curly leaf kale, stems removed and roughly chopped

4 garlic cloves

½ teaspoon kosher salt

Freshly cracked black pepper

FOR THE PANINI:

6 ounces gruyere, shredded

4 soft small ciabatta style bread rolls

Note: For optimal panini, the type of bread you use is important. The bread's crust should be soft, not too textured or crispy, and the bread not too thick. Don't use traditional ciabatta. Look for a rectangular wide, flat, elongated roll, or Italian-style bread that will squish well when pressed.

All of the elements of these tasty little sandwiches can be prepped ahead, making them excellent casual dinner party fare when paired with a soup or salad. Crisp up the pancetta and cook the kale with plenty of garlic, and make the sweet and savory tomato jam, spiced with cumin, ginger and smoked paprika. It is a killer condiment, melding in the most incredible way with the braised kale and earthy gruyere cheese.

1. Make the tomato jam. Combine all of the ingredients for the jam in a medium saucepan. Bring to a simmer, partially covering to protect from splatters, and cook for about 35-45 minutes, stirring occasionally. It should be very thick, like a chunky jam. *This will keep for a week in the refrigerator.*

2. For the kale, pour the oil into a large skillet. Fry the pancetta over medium-high heat until crispy, keeping an eye on it so it doesn't burn, and stirring often. Remove to a paper towel lined plate using a slotted spoon. If there is a lot of fat left in the skillet, drain off all but about 1 tablespoon. Reduce the heat to low, and add the kale, garlic and the smoked paprika. Cook until the kale is soft, about 8 minutes, stirring occasionally. If it is dry, add a little water to the pan to help soften the kale, but make sure it cooks off and the kale is not too moist before using it in the panini.

3. Split your panini breads and spread the tomato jam on the top halves. Sprinkle bottom halves with half of the cheese, and divide the kale evenly among the bottom halves. Divide the pancetta equally between the sandwiches, laying it evenly over the kale. Finally, sprinkle the remaining cheese on top of the kale/pancetta, and place the top halves on the sandwiches.

4. Heat a panini pan, skillet or grill to medium. Brush a little olive oil onto the pan and cook the sandwiches, flipping once, until heated through and the cheese has melted. If not using a panini pan, push down on the sandwiches while cooking to flatten. You could also use a heavy cast iron skillet to help press the panini. Cut in half and serve hot.

HOT EGGPLANT SANDWICH WITH GOAT CHEESE AND A FRIED EGG

Picture steaming hot eggplant braised in a tomato basil sauce, nestled in a chewy ciabatta roll, with slowly melting goat cheese. Now, top that with a perfectly fried egg, yellow gold dripping down the sides, with a decadence that only runny yolks can yield. This is my favorite kind of sandwich... seriously messy! Even eggplant skeptics get behind this one - it turned my son into an eggplant lover. A little dollop of harissa is optional, but encouraged. Go spicy if you can handle the heat.

Makes 4 sandwiches

3-4 tablespoons extra virgin olive oil	1 teaspoon kosher salt
1 large eggplant (about 1 pound)	4 ounces fresh goat cheese
1 tablespoon unsweetened cocoa powder	4 eggs
4 garlic cloves, chopped	Pat of butter or a little oil for frying the eggs
14 ounce can diced tomatoes	4 teaspoons jarred harissa sauce, mild or hot, optional
¼ cup loosely packed basil, chopped	4 square ciabatta style rolls, halved horizontally
1 teaspoon sugar	

1. Preheat your oven to 300 F.

2. Slice the eggplant about ¼" thick. Lay out on your cutting board or work surface, and sprinkle a little salt on the tops. Place the cocoa in a small, fine mesh sieve, and dust the eggplant slices with half of the cocoa. If you do not have a sieve, you can sprinkle the cocoa using your fingertips. Warm the oil over medium heat in a large skillet. Place the eggplant in the oil, cocoa side down, then sprinkle the remaining cocoa and another sprinkle of salt over the sides facing up. Fry without moving for 2 minutes, then turn them over and fry the other sides. You may need to do this in batches, adding more oil to the pan each time.

3. Remove the eggplant to a plate. It may not be fully cooked and that's ok. Add the tomatoes, garlic and basil to the skillet, and adjust the heat so that it comes to a low simmer. Scrape up any bits sticking to the bottom of the pan, and season with the salt and sugar, stirring to combine. Return the eggplant to the pan, nestling in the sauce and overlapping them if necessary. Cover the skillet, turn the heat to low and cook for 8 minutes. Flip the eggplant over, return the lid, and cook for another few minutes, until the eggplant is fully cooked and the tomatoes are thickened. If the tomato sauce is not thick, remove the lid and increase the heat to cook it down. There should be less liquid than a tomato sauce for pasta, otherwise your sandwiches will be too wet. Keep warm over low heat once it is the right consistency.

4. Lay the rolls out, cut side up, on a baking sheet and crumble the goat cheese on the bottom halves. Place in the warm oven (or toaster oven) while you cook the eggs.

5. Place a large, non-stick skillet over medium heat with a little butter, about a half tablespoon. Carefully

crack the eggs into the skillet and turn the heat to low. Cook for a few minutes until they set up, then carefully flip them without breaking the yolk. Let them cook for 30 seconds on the second side. Of course, if you don't like a runny yolk, cook the eggs longer or break the yolks.

6. Remove the rolls from the oven and spoon the eggplant on the bottom halves of the rolls with the goat cheese, then top each with an egg and a teaspoon of the harissa, if using. Serve right away.

Depending on the size of your eggplant, you may have leftover filling. Use what looks like an appropriate amount to you for each sandwich, 2 or 3 pieces of eggplant and some sauce.

ALMOST A DÖNER WRAP - MEDITERRANEAN STYLE

Makes 2 wraps

1 small cooked chicken breast

½ cup tomato, seeded and diced

½ cup crumbled feta

¼ cup chopped roasted bell pepper, store bought or homemade

¼ cup kalamata olives, pitted and halved

½ cup shredded cabbage or romaine lettuce

½ cup hummus, store bought or homemade

¼ cup store bought crunchy chickpeas

2 large lavash flatbreads

FOR THE TZATZIKI:

1 small garlic clove, grated on a microplane

1 tablespoon fresh lemon juice

¼ cup grated cucumber

¼ cup plain Greek yogurt

1 tablespoon fresh dill, chopped (or substitute fresh mint)

½ teaspoon kosher salt

My hubby believes the success of this sandwich lies in how thinly you slice the meat. Important for sure, but the layering of flavors does it for me. At first glance, it may look like a long list for a wrap, but it's pretty simple to put together. Organizing your ingredients, known as *mise-en-place*, before beginning to assemble the wraps will streamline the operation. I set up my counter like an assembly line. Chickpeas provide a great salty crunch that will make you want to keep munching! They come in lots of different flavors; here, a simple salted chickpea is best.

Notes: Lavash is a middle eastern flatbread, and when it's not in stock in the fresh bread aisle, I'll often find it in the freezer section. In a pinch, I've made these on burrito-sized tortillas, which is a fine substitution.

You can buy a small, pre-cooked chicken breast, or roast your own. If you are cooking it at home, I recommend seasoning the breast with olive oil, salt and a dusting of cumin and paprika. Roast in a preheated oven at 350 F for 15 minutes or until cooked through. Let it rest for a few minutes before slicing.

1. Make the tzatziki. Place the grated garlic in a small bowl with the lemon juice and let it sit for a minute or two. *This helps take the raw sharpness from the garlic.* Stir in the cucumber, yogurt, dill and salt. *The tzatziki can be made up to a day ahead of time.*

2. Slice the chicken breast as thin as you possibly can. Combine the tomato, feta, bell pepper, and olives in a small bowl. Ready your cabbage or lettuce, chickpeas and tzatziki.

3. Assemble one wrap at a time. Spread half of the hummus on the bottom half of one lavash. Lay half of the chicken across the lavash, then top with half of the tomato mixture, half the cabbage and crunchy chickpeas. Dollop about 2 tablespoons of the tzatziki over top. Roll like a burrito, folding the ends in as you roll so that the filling doesn't fall out of the bottom. For an authentic feel, wrap in parchment paper and tape to secure, then cut the sandwich in half lengthwise. Repeat with the other lavash, and serve with extra tzatziki.

SALMON BÁNH MI

Makes 2 sandwiches

2 medium carrots

½ lime, zest plus juice

1 tablespoon fish sauce

2 teaspoons coconut sugar or granulated sugar

8 ounces cooked salmon, broken into large flaked pieces

1 medium jalapeño, seeded and sliced lengthwise into strips, optional

2 small, soft french style rolls (or a larger soft baguette cut into 8" lengths)

2-3 tablespoons mayonnaise

3-inch piece of cucumber, peeled, seeded and sliced thinly

½ cup washed cilantro, very roughly chopped

2 tablespoons sriracha sauce

Note: Certain supermarkets sell cooked salmon at their deli counter. If you can't find this, you can easily cook your own at home. Roast the salmon, sprinkled with a little salt, in a 350 F oven for 10-12 minutes. Exact time will depend on the type and thickness of the salmon you buy. Roast it on a piece of aluminum foil for easy clean up. High quality canned salmon is also an acceptable alternative.

Originating in Vietnam, the bánh mi is a culmination of French colonial influences on classic Vietnamese flavors. Highly seasoned ingredients are nestled into a crunchy french baguette, and traditionally includes a smear of pâté. The popularity of bánh mi has soared in our country in the past decade or so, and you can find them filled with everything from pork to sardines to chicken or tofu. Mine uses salmon, and I've simplified the recipe so that it's easy to make at home, but will have you feeling like you're huddled outside a trendy food truck... without the lines, of course! There are so many big, bold flavors in this sandwich, though it's the sriracha, a bottled chili sauce with a spicy kick, which brings them all together.

1. Begin by making the carrot salad. Shred the carrot on the large holes of a box grater. You should end up with a little less than a cup. Place the shredded carrot in a bowl, then zest the lime into the bowl. Add the juice from the half lime, then the fish sauce and sugar. Stir to combine.

2. Split the rolls in half lengthwise. Smear a layer of mayo on the bottom of the rolls, then lay the cucumber slices on top of the mayo. Add equal amounts of the salmon to each sandwich, top with the carrot salad, including some of the juice, cilantro and jalapeño, if using, and finally drizzle with the sriracha sauce. Serve immediately.

SMOKED TROUT, HEIRLOOM TOMATO & WHIPPED TARRAGON GOAT CHEESE TARTINE

Serves 4

4 ounces soft goat cheese

¼ cup half and half or cream

2 teaspoons fresh lemon juice

½ teaspoon kosher salt

1 tablespoon fresh tarragon, coarsely chopped

3-4 medium tomatoes (about 1 pound), seeded and cut into rough chunks about ½"

8 ounces smoked trout, broken into large flaky pieces

2 scallions (green onion), roughly chopped

1 tablespoon capers

Freshly cracked black pepper

4 slices good sourdough bread, about ½" thick

1 clove garlic, cut in half

A tartine is a classic French dish, essentially an open faced sandwich. Served with a knife and a fork, it can be topped with just about anything, sweet or savory. Make this tartine when heirloom tomatoes are at their peak. Sweet and juicy, there's nothing like a perfectly ripe summer tomato, especially paired with creamy, whipped goat cheese. You'll want to schmear this spread on everything- and you should! Make a double batch and try it on bagels, or as a dip for veggies, or a spread for crackers. But it is heaven in this tartine. Spread thickly on a big slice of sourdough bread, topped with the tomatoes, smoky trout, green onions and capers, it's hard to think of a more perfect lunch.

1. Place the goat cheese, half and half, lemon juice and salt, in a mini food processor. Blend for a minute or two until thickened and totally creamy, scraping down the sides once or twice. Add the tarragon and pulse a few times to blend. *If you don't have a mini food processor, use electric beaters to whip it together.*

2. Toast the bread so it just takes on a slight color. You don't want it to be too crispy. It should be soft in the middle and crisp on the edges. As soon as it comes out of the toaster, rub the cut piece of garlic on each slice. *This gives a hint of garlic flavor without it being overpowering.* Spread an equal amount of the goat cheese mixture on each slice, then divide the tomato and trout evenly between the bread. Sprinkle with the onion and capers, and top with freshly cracked black pepper. Serve with a knife and fork.

5 O'CLOCK SOMEWHERE: SNACKS & COCKTAILS

I am a firm believer that the intro to the meal should whet the appetite, not sabotage it. Little bites over happy hour are a requirement, but they shouldn't fill you up so much that you cannot enjoy the main event.

Nor should they require a ton of attention by the host. This is the time to use that cute little jar of pepper jam your friend brought as a hostess gift. Or to whip up a quick dip in your food processor. This is the time to smear some soft cheese on crusty toasts, topped with a sliver of fruit and a drizzle of honey, served alongside olives, or a jar of something pickled. Or a few scoops of spiced nuts, which you have on hand for entertaining.

When hosting a cocktail hour with friends, you might prefer something more substantial. I've included a few recipes that require a bit more cooking. They also make the perfect "wow" plate for when you're asked to bring an hors d'oeuvre to share. Or a nice light dinner when served alongside a salad.

Each appetizer you'll find paired with a cocktail designed to compliment the flavors and spirit of the dish - though each bite and drink will also easily stand on their own, so you needn't stick to the formula. Lots of credit goes to my husband, Justin, for his collaboration in this section. He is our resident mixologist and has an instinct for making perfectly balanced cocktails.

WHIPPED FETA DIP WITH MINT CHILI OIL

Makes about 2 cups – *enjoy with Unbridled Spirit*

FOR THE DIP:

8 ounces feta

½ cup plain Greek yogurt

1 large garlic clove, grated finely or crushed

1 tablespoon lemon juice

Zest from ½ of the lemon

¼ teaspoon kosher salt

FOR THE CHILI OIL:

3 tablespoons extra virgin olive oil

1 tablespoon chopped mint, or use 1 teaspoon dried mint

1 teaspoon red pepper flakes

⅛ teaspoon kosher salt

FOR SERVING:

Pita, naan or cut vegetables

Everybody needs a simple cheese dip in their repertoire. My whipped feta is just what you'd expect - creamy, tangy and fresh tasting from the hit of lemon. The zesty appears in the form of chili oil flecked with mint. Not only a welcome color contrast to the stark white dip, but an incredibly flavorful oil that will keep your soft flatbread dipping in for more.

1. Place all of the ingredients for the dip in a food processor and blend until creamy. Transfer it to a wide, shallow bowl for serving, and using the back of a spoon create a swirl design in the dip.

2. Combine the ingredients for the chili oil in a small bowl. Pour over the whipped feta, allowing it to pool in the swirls you created. *This can be refrigerated for a few hours, covered, but let it sit out for 15 minutes before serving to take the chill off.*

3. To serve, warm the naan or pita in a low oven or toaster for a few minutes. Cut or tear into pieces and place on a serving plate with the bowl of feta dip.

UNBRIDLED SPIRIT

Makes 1 drink

1 ½ ounces (3 tbsp) Aperol®

1 ½ ounces (3 tbsp) bourbon

½ ounce (1 tbsp) fresh lemon juice

1 ounce (2 tbsp) ginger beer

OPTIONAL GARNISH:

Lemon twist or slice of lemon, fresh herbs such as mint or basil

Any time is a good time for a refreshing bourbon cocktail! Here, Aperol adds sweetness, while the lemon provides acidity and the ginger beer spices things up with its fun pop of effervescence!

1. Combine the Aperol, bourbon, and lemon juice in a short glass and stir to combine. Add lots of ice and top with ginger beer. Stir gently. Garnish if desired.

TUNA PÂTÉ WITH SUNDRIED TOMATOES

Makes about 2 cups – *enjoy with The Hugo*

1 cup canned cannellini beans, rinsed and drained well

½ cup albacore tuna packed in olive oil (3.2 ounces)

1 tablespoon chopped rosemary

1 tablespoon fresh lemon juice

½ teaspoon lemon zest

1 garlic clove, crushed or grated

½ teaspoon kosher salt

Freshly cracked black pepper

¼ cup extra virgin olive oil

FOR SERVING:

Crackers

⅓ cup sundried tomatoes in olive oil, cut into bite sized pieces, if large

A bowl of marinated olives

Cut vegetables, optional

Here's how I serve this - as an antipasto platter, letting guests assemble their own snacks. A dish full of olives, a bowl of sun dried tomatoes in olive oil, a smattering of crackers... and the star of the show, tuna and white bean pâté. Add a few carrot and celery sticks, and fresh cherry tomatoes, and dinner snacks are done! But back to the tuna - I love a good fish spread, though frequently they are too weighed down by cream cheese or mayo. Here, white beans produce a smooth and creamy dip, highlighted by fresh rosemary, garlic and lemon, and topped with sun dried tomato for pop. My twist on an old school classic!

1. Puree the cannellini beans in a food processor for a minute or two, scraping down the sides to make sure that the mixture is creamy. Add all of the remaining ingredients, except for the olive oil, and process for 2 minutes. With the motor running, pour in the olive oil in a steady stream, then let the machine run for another minute. Scrape into a serving bowl.

2. Arrange a serving platter with the bowl of tuna pate, a bowl of the sun dried tomatoes, the crackers, olives, and cut vegetables, if using.

THE HUGO

Makes 2 drinks

10 ounces (1 ¼ cup) Prosecco

4 ounces (½ cup) elderflower liqueur, such as St. Germain®

8 or 10 fresh mint leaves

4 ounces (½ cup) seltzer water

Slice of lime for garnish

Bubbly, light and refreshing, this to me is a perfect pre-dinner cocktail. I am a big fan of spritz drinks, as they are typically low-alcohol and incredibly tasty. I have long loved the popular Aperol Spritz, and discovered its cousin, the classic, Hugo, while on vacation a few years ago. It quickly became one of my new favorites!

1. Divide the mint into two large wine glasses and add 2 ounces of the elderflower liqueur to each glass. Fill the glasses with ice, then pour 5 ounces of prosecco into each glass. Stir gently, then add two ounces of the seltzer water to each glass. Garnish with a slice of lime and serve.

ROSEMARY ROASTED MIXED NUTS

Makes 2 lbs – *enjoy with Gingery Hot Spiked Apple Cider*

8 ounces (1 cup) raw pecans

8 ounces (1 cup) raw almonds

8 ounces (1 cup) raw cashews

4 ounces (½ cup) raw brazil nuts

4 ounces (½ cup) raw pistachios

2 tablespoons light brown sugar

1 tablespoon kosher salt

1 tablespoon chopped fresh rosemary

4 tablespoons unsalted butter

1 tablespoon honey

Note: Any mixture of nuts will do, as long as you have 2 pounds total.

About a decade ago, I started making mixed nuts around the holidays. The first batch disappeared in a few days, so I decided big batches were a must. Scaling up doesn't add much effort and has so many benefits! Now, every November I make a TON and store them in baggies in the freezer. Not only do I pull them out for easy apps on entertaining nights, they make the perfect holiday hostess gift. Just place in a food-safe cellophane bag, tie off with raffia and voila! Keep a good amount for yourself, though, as they are a fairly addictive snack, and add a hearty crunch when chopped and sprinkled on fresh salads or roasted vegetables.

1. Preheat your oven to 275 F. Combine the nuts, brown sugar, salt and rosemary in a bowl.

2. Melt the butter in a small pan, and let it cook over medium heat until the milk solids turn brown. It will bubble and pop while it's cooking, stir gently with a silicone spatula, and remove from the heat as soon as you see the butter starting to brown. It can burn very quickly. Stir in the honey, then pour it over the nuts and mix until the nuts are evenly coated.

3. Transfer to a parchment lined baking sheet and bake for 30-35 minutes, stirring every 10 minutes and rotating the pan halfway through. Let cool completely, then store at room temperature for 2 weeks, or in the freezer for 2 months.

GINGERY HOT SPIKED APPLE CIDER

Makes 2 drinks

16 ounces (2 cups) apple cider

1 small cinnamon stick

2 ounces (¼ cup) dark rum

2 ounces (¼ cup) ginger liqueur,
such as Domaine de Canton®

1 ounce (2 tbsp) orange juice

1 teaspoons maple syrup

OPTIONAL GARNISHES:

Apples slices, cinnamon stick,
star anise

My husband and I were standing around the kitchen, contemplating an apple-y rum drink to go with mixed nuts. We knew we wanted holiday-inspired flavors, like ginger and orange... then he had the clever idea, "What if we make it *hot*?" Ginger and spice and everything nice only gets better sipped warm and cozy from a mug.

1. Pour the apple cider in a medium saucepan and add the cinnamon stick. Simmer for 2 minutes until reduced by roughly ¼. Remove from the heat and discard the cinnamon stick.

2. Stir in the orange juice and maple syrup, then away from heat or open flame, stir in the rum and ginger liqueur. Stir gently, then ladle into mugs and serve warm with the apple slices.

For a larger gathering, you can scale the recipe up and make it in a slow cooker. Add all ingredients and heat the mixture on medium for 1 hour. Ladle into mugs and serve warm with an apple wedge for garnish.

FRESH APRICOT GORGONZOLA CROSTINI

Serves 4 – *enjoy with Summertime Aperitivo*

12 pieces of thinly sliced baguette, toasted, or use store-bought crostini toasts

3 ripe apricots

4 ounces gorgonzola

Honey for drizzling

12 basil leaves for garnish

A sprinkle of flaky sea salt and freshly ground black pepper

Note: In a pinch, a nice ripe peach is a good substitute if you can't find good apricots.

I find crostini to be the ultimate non-recipe appetizer. In the winter, I might reach for a jar of fig jam and whatever cheese I have in the fridge. In the summer, I'll use fresh fruit, cured meat and a soft brie. Smoked mackerel, fresh herbs and lemon? Yum. Fresh pea and mint pesto with a dollop of ricotta... I could go on and on, possibilities are limitless. Certain crostini combos I find myself revisiting frequently, like this one. We adore apricots. When they are good, they are great! Robust Italian cheese pairs perfectly, with the creamy gorgonzola cutting the tartness of the fruit. But the real star is the honey, bridging the divide. It highlights the sweetness in the fruit, and counterbalances the saltiness of the cheese. This is a wonderfully seasonal and simple app.

1. Lay the bread on a serving platter. Divide the cheese evenly among the toasts, taking advantage of gorgonzola's creaminess and spreading it into the toast. Pit the apricots and cut each into 4 wedges. Lay one wedge on top of each toast, then drizzle with a generous amount of honey, crack fresh black pepper over top and sprinkle with the salt. Top each toast with a basil leaf. If your leaves are large, tear them into smaller pieces to fit the toasts.

SUMMERTIME APERITIVO

Makes 1 drink

6 ounces (¾ cup) white wine, such as a Sauvignon Blanc, unoaked Chardonnay, Albarino or Pinot Grigio

1 ounce (2 tbsp) Lillet® Blanc

1 ounce (2 tbsp) Crème de Cassis

1 teaspoon fresh lemon juice

A few blackberries and strawberries, or whatever fresh fruit you have on hand

Late summer afternoons, I can usually be found sipping a version of this drink while milling about the kitchen gathering my thoughts for the evening's meal. Born from having leftover white wine, though while still completely drinkable, has lost some of its luster. It's often a no-recipe drink - maybe a splash of elderflower liqueur and a bit of Aperol, a few squeezes of citrus, a few fresh summer berries, and always tons of ice. In this version, Lillet blanc and cassis bring the zest, brightened by fresh lemon juice. A crisper, drier white, like a sauvignon blanc or unoaked chardonnay, is best, but really most anything will do!

1. Pour the wine in a white wine glass. Add Lillet, Creme de Cassis and the lemon juice. Give it a swirl, then add plenty of ice. Toss in the berries or fruit and serve.

CREAMY TOMATILLO AVOCADO DIP

Serves 8 as an appetizer – *enjoy with One Tequila, Two Tequila*

1 large ripe hass avocado

10 ounces tomatillos (about 8 large), papery husk removed and rinsed

1 small white onion, peeled and cut into ½" rounds

4 large garlic cloves, peel left on

1 jalapeño

¼ cup cilantro

1 tablespoon fresh lime juice

1 teaspoon kosher salt

Tortilla chips for serving

This creamy, superbly flavorful salsa has so much potential... it can be anything you want it to be. Here, it serves as an appetizer, with chips for dipping. It also makes a fantastic salsa for tacos, a terrific topping for burritos or nachos and I've even used it as a salad dressing with crisp romaine! As it contains fresh avocado, it's best the day it's made - however, with the acidity of the tomatillos, it will keep for 2-3 days in the fridge.

1. Place the tomatillos, onion, garlic and jalapeño in a cast iron skillet or baking dish large enough to hold them in one layer. If using a baking dish, lay a sheet of parchment or foil brushed with oil on the bottom. Broil the vegetables about 6-8 inches from the heat until slightly charred, then turn them and char the other side. It should take about 8 minutes per side, but keep an eye on it in case your broiler is very hot. Be careful of the garlic - it can overcook easily. If the cloves are on the smaller side, you might take them out after only 6 minutes.

2. Peel the garlic, and seed and stem the jalapeño. Place the jalapeño, garlic, onion, tomatillos and salt in a blender and puree. Be careful if they are still very hot, as the built up heat can cause the top to pop off the blender. Keep a firm hand on it. I like to put a dish towel over top as well to prevent any splatters.

3. Halve the avocado, remove the pit and scoop the flesh into the blender along with the cilantro and lime, and puree again. Taste for seasoning and add more salt, if necessary. Serve with chips or jicama, or use on tacos or burritos. *The salsa is best within a few hours of being made, but will keep well for a day or two in the refrigerator.*

ONE TEQUILA, TWO TEQUILA

Makes 1 drink

1 ounce (2 tbsp) silver tequila

¾ ounce (1 ½ tbsp) mezcal

¾ ounce (1 ½ tbsp) elderflower liqueur, such as St. Germain®

½ ounce (1 tbsp) Aperol®

1 ¼ ounce (2 tbsp plus 1 tsp) orange juice

½ ounce (1 tbsp) lime juice

This drink has been a long time favorite of mine - and the name dates back to its origin. Given that mezcal is agave-based, I once thought it simply to be a type of tequila, and named this drink based on that assumption. In actuality, all tequila is a type of mezcal, BUT not all mezcal is categorized as tequila! You see, any of 50 species of agave can be used to make mezcal, and only one type can be used to make tequila. Tequila also has a particular denomination of origin and is distilled using a different technique from other mezcal. Sounds confusing, but the bottom line is this... this drink is so yum, it doesn't really matter what you call it!

1. Combine all the ingredients in a cocktail shaker filled with ice. Shake vigorously, then strain into a glass filled with ice.

PROSCIUTTO WRAPPED ROASTED PEARS

Serves 4 – *enjoy with Autumn Negroni*

1 large bosc pear, firm but ripe

5 or 6 slices of prosciutto

2-ish ounces young manchego cheese

Honey for drizzling

Freshly cracked black pepper and flaky sea salt for finishing

Note: Pears can be prepared ahead of time through step 2 and refrigerated, however, they could brown slightly on the edges if they sit for more than an hour or two before baking.

Wrapping any sweet fruit in salty prosciutto is almost like cheating. It's too delicious to be so easy. Fresh figs are one of my favorites, but their season is short. When I can find figs, I halve them, put a dab of blue cheese on the cut side, wrap it in prosciutto and bake until soft and juicy. Pure heaven. Pears are much easier to come by, and equally as heavenly when paired with a nutty manchego cheese. While the pears and cheese soften in the oven, the prosciutto crisps and intensifies, creating a symphony of textures and flavors.

1. Preheat your oven (or toaster oven) to 350 F. Line a small baking sheet with parchment paper.

2. Halve and core the pears. Slice thinly lengthwise, about ⅛-inch thick. Cut the manchego cheese into wedges, slightly smaller than the pear slices. You want the pear to be the dominant flavor, and the cheese to be an accent. Tear the prosciutto into 3 or 4 pieces per slice, and wrap a small piece around the pear and cheese. You don't want to have too much prosciutto, but it should be enough that it wraps around fully, holding the cheese and pear together. Place them on the prepared baking sheet.

3. Bake the pears for about 10 minutes. The prosciutto should crisp up slightly. The cheese will not melt and ooze - it should keep its shape. Remove from the oven, drizzle with honey and sprinkle a little flaky salt and freshly cracked black pepper. Serve warm.

AUTUMN NEGRONI

Makes 1 drink

1 ½ ounces (3 tbsp) Campari®

1 ½ ounces (3 tbsp) sweet Vermouth

1 ounce (2 tbsp) Calvados, or other apple or pear brandy

A strip of orange zest

Campari is one of those flavors that people downright love, or approach with skepticism. It is bitter to be sure - though, to me, so nicely balanced by its sweetness, adding perfect structure and a distinct profile to cocktails. I love it. And I love how popular the Negroni has become in recent years. A classic Italian drink, and one that packs a punch, the Negroni is made from equal parts of Campari, gin and sweet vermouth. My autumnal version swaps the gin for Calvados, a french apple brandy. With a hint of orange and an apple slice for garnish, it's a stellar fall-inspired libation.

1. Combine the Campari, vermouth, and calvados in a glass. Stir gently, and add plenty of ice and the orange peel. Garnish with an apple slice, if using.

HONEY RICOTTA NAAN WITH ROASTED CAULIFLOWER

Serves 8 as an appetizer – *enjoy with Lexi's G&T*

1 small cauliflower (1 ¼ pounds)

1 teaspoon garam masala

¼ teaspoon cumin seeds

2 tablespoons olive oil

1 ½ teaspoons kosher salt

2 garlic cloves, chopped finely

¼ cup golden raisins

½ cup plus 2 tablespoons ricotta

1 ½ tablespoons honey

4 purchased naan flatbreads

2 tablespoons fresh mint, chopped

2 tablespoons oiled cured black olives, pitted and halved

Nowhere near traditional, this flatbread nods to Indian cuisine. Garam masala is a wonderfully aromatic spice blend and adds so much flavor - I find it especially nice paired with roasted cauliflower. Golden raisins add a hint of sweetness, and the cheese creates a pillowy bed that binds it all together. Your guests will find these bites an unexpected, delicious foray to the meal - or you may choose to serve these flatbreads as a main, paired with a fresh, green salad. Roasting of the cauliflower adds a bit more prep time than many of my appetizers, but the elements can be done ahead, and flatbreads assembled just before baking.

1. Preheat your oven to 375 F. Remove the core from the cauliflower and discard, then cut the florets into small pieces (¾ inch). Place the florets in a roasting dish large enough to hold without crowding and toss with the olive oil, garam masala, cumin and salt. Roast, stirring once or twice, until soft and cooked through about 20-25 minutes. Remove from the oven and stir in the garlic and raisins while it is still hot. Reduce the oven temperature to 325.

2. Mix the ricotta, honey, a pinch of salt and plenty of black pepper in a small bowl.

3. Place the 4 naan breads on two baking pans. Divide the ricotta mixture between the four breads spreading evenly, and then distribute the cauliflower over top. Scatter the olives on the cauliflower, and place in the oven. Bake for 8 minutes then remove to a serving plate or wood board and sprinkle with the fresh mint. Cut each flatbread into 6 pieces and serve.

LEXI'S G&T

Makes 1 drink

2 ounces (¼ cup) gin

1 ½ ounces (3 tbsp) fresh grapefruit juice

3 ounces (¼ cup plus 2 tbsp) tonic water

Sliced cucumber or fresh mint for garnish

When I was a kid growing up in Florida, my siblings and I would play outside A LOT, and usually without shoes on. It happened on occasion that one of us would find ourselves obliviously standing on an ant pile, and before we knew it, fire ants were halfway up our legs. After a frantic dash to the house, and a good hose-down, my mom would always get out the gin and rub it on our legs. Whether it was a true medicinal cure, or helpful placebo, it didn't take long for the sting to abate. This, I credit for my affinity to the herbaceous elixir. My favorite G&T is a model of simplicity, only as good as the sum of its parts. Likewise, here, freshly squeezed juice and good gin is a must. Despite the influx of excellent craft gins, for this drink I reach for a classic - Beefeater, an oldy but a goody. But use your favorite brand and it will be sure to please.

1. Fill a tall glass with ice. Add the gin, juice and tonic and stir gently to combine. Garnish with a slice of cucumber or a few mint leaves and enjoy.

SWEET & SPICY ASIAN SHRIMP

Serves 4 as an appetizer – *enjoy with Cherry Ginger Vodka Cooler*

1 pound large shrimp, peeled with tail on and deveined

¼ cup coconut sugar

1 large jalapeño, seeded and chopped

2 tablespoons fish sauce

4 garlic cloves, grated or chopped very finely

¼ teaspoon kosher salt

2 tablespoons neutral oil, such as canola or grapeseed oil

¼ cup fresh basil leaves, torn into pieces

½ lime

Note: You never know what you're going to get with jalapeños. They could be incredibly spicy, or very mild. You might want to taste your chili to gauge how much you want to use depending on your preference for spice level.

People. Like. Shrimp. Like, a ton. Statistics say Americans eat on average 4 pounds per person per year. Once you try this Asian-inspired shrimp app, you may never look twice at shrimp cocktail. Sweet and spicy, with a few dashes of fish sauce for umami, these shrimp are a hit. Serve with toothpicks or small appetizer plates and forks - or portioned for dinner over steamed rice.

1. Mix together the coconut sugar, jalapeño, fish sauce, garlic and salt. Add the shrimp and marinate for 15 minutes.

2. Pour the oil in a large skillet and place over medium-high heat. The pan should be very hot, but not smoking. Add the shrimp, leaving the marinade behind. *If you cannot fit them all in without crowding, do them in batches.* Cook the shrimp about a minute per side, however, the exact cook time will depend on the size of your shrimp. It is important not to overcook them or else they will be rubbery, not tender. Remove to a serving platter.

3. Pour the marinade into the pan and cook over medium-high heat for 1-2 minutes until just slightly reduced. Pour the sauce over the shrimp, sprinkle with the basil, and squeeze the fresh lime juice over everything.

CHERRY GINGER VODKA COOLER

Makes 1 drink

1 ½ ounces (3 tbsp) vodka

¾ ounce (1 ½ tbsp) ginger liqueur, such as Domaine de Canton®

½ ounce (1 tbsp) grenadine

3 fresh or frozen cherries

¼ ounce (½ tbsp) fresh lime juice

This refreshing summer sipper is so smooth, it's the kind of cocktail that can sneak up on you. Cherries and ginger are a nod to the Asian flavors in the shrimp appetizer, and of course vodka is a blank slate for the sweet fruit and spiced liqueur. Rounded out with a splash of grenadine and fresh lime, it's an easy going cooler.

1. Place two cherries in a cocktail shaker and mash with a muddler until slightly broken down. Add the vodka, ginger liqueur, grenadine and lime juice and a handful of ice. Shake vigorously, then strain into a coup glass. Garnish with a whole cherry.

HARISSA LAMB QUESADILLAS WITH LIME CREMA

Serves 8-10 as an appetizer –
enjoy with Mexican 75

FOR THE QUESADILLAS:

6 ounces ground lamb

¼ cup chopped white onion

¾ cup chopped cremini mushrooms

2 garlic cloves, chopped

1 teaspoon ground cumin

1 teaspoon dried oregano

¾ teaspoon kosher salt

½ cup jarred harissa, mild or spicy

2 cups shredded cheese, a mixture of smoked cheddar and mozzarella or all mozzarella

6 flour tortillas, 8" size

2-3 teaspoons olive oil

FOR THE LIME CREAM:

½ cup sour cream

1 tablespoon fresh lime juice

½ teaspoon lime zest

⅛ teaspoon kosher salt

Note: If you don't enjoy lamb, you can substitute ground turkey. You will need to saute the turkey in olive oil as it does not have the same fat content as the lamb. To make a vegetarian version, increase the mushrooms to ½ pound, making sure to cook all of their liquid off before adding the harissa.

It's easy to forget about quesadillas as an appetizer option; they are so often served as a heartier dinner entree. But, cut into little triangles and served with a lime crema sauce, quesadillas are perfect party fare. Years ago when I worked in the catering department at Dean & Deluca in Washington, D.C., one of the most popular passed appetizers at parties around the capitol were quesadillas - such a crowd pleaser! And these are sure to be a hit at your next gathering. Umami-packed spiced lamb, mushrooms and gooey cheese, are all set off by the piquant harissa. This jarred red pepper condiment melds beautifully, providing a necessary acidity to balance the richness of lamb.

1. Saute the lamb and chopped onions with ½ teaspoon salt in a medium skillet over medium-high. Cook, stirring to break up the lamb, until cooked through. Drain and discard any extra fat, then add the garlic, mushrooms, remaining ¼ teaspoon salt and spices and cook another 2-3 minutes, stirring frequently. Stir in the harissa and scrape up any bits sticking to the bottom, cooking until just warmed through, about 1-2 minutes. *Lamb can be cooked ahead of time and refrigerated until ready to use.*

2. Make the lime cream by combining all the ingredients in a small bowl.

3. Warm a cast iron or nonstick skillet over medium heat and pour a teaspoon of olive oil on the bottom. Place one tortilla in the skillet, top with ⅓ cup of cheese, then ⅓ of the lamb mixture. Top with another ⅓ cup of cheese and then another tortilla and cook for 1-2 minutes until browned on the bottom. Carefully flip the tortilla over to cook the other side. *It can be easiest to do this by sliding it onto a plate, then inverting the pan over the plate and flipping it back over.* Repeat with the remaining ingredients, making 3 quesadillas.

4. To serve, cut the tortillas into 6 wedges each (18 total), and place on a serving plate with a bowl of the lime cream. *The lime cream can be drizzled over the quesadillas if you plan to serve them with appetizer plates and forks.*

Quesadillas can be cooked and kept warm in a low oven, uncut, for 10-15 minutes, covered with a piece of foil so that the tortillas do not dry out.

MEXICAN 75

Makes 1 drink

1 ounce (2 tbsp) tequila

½ ounce (1 tbsp) fresh lime juice

2 teaspoons agave

4 ounces (1 cup) sparkling wine, chilled

Note: Simple syrup may be used in place of the agave. Combine equal parts sugar and water and warm until sugar is dissolved. Let cool before using.

Ever hear of the classic cocktail, a French 75? It's tall, slender and elegant - a sophisticated drink of gin, sparkling wine, simple syrup and lemon, served in a champagne flute. I don't have them often, but it is a favorite of mine on a special occasion. A few summers ago, I was making a Mexican-inspired dinner for friends, and wanted to serve a fun, themed drink that was *not* a margarita. I had a bottle of prosecco in the fridge, and remembered my love for the classic French 75. Working from there, I did this riff and dubbed it the Mexican 75... using lime instead of lemon, and tequila instead of gin. Dare I say, I might even like it better! Using agave syrup is a natural match with the tequila in the recipe, but you can also make a simple syrup if you don't have agave. Footnote, I've since come to realize that others have had a similar epiphany! Great minds, so they say. My version uses slightly different proportions then ones I've seen.

1. Combine the tequila, lime juice and agave and stir to combine. Pour into a champagne flute or wine glass, then top with the sparkling wine.

NOODLES & DOUGH

Some mains are perfectly fine served luke-warm - their flavors may even peak at this temperature. Pizza and pasta are decidedly *NOT* these dishes... they wait for no one. Serve them hot, as soon as they are ready. If others are late to the table, that's their problem. You have permission to begin. Tell them I said so :)

I encourage you to review my pasta making tips on page **16**; these methods are not just helpful, but vital to the success of a pasta dish.

As for pizza, a word about dough. I chose not to include my dough recipes in the book, however, you will find them on my website should you wish to make your own. Nowadays, many grocers sell fresh pizza dough in the refrigerated section. I am not talking about pre-baked crust - but instead, raw dough for you to stretch, form and top. Allow it to come to room temperature before getting started, which makes it easier to work with. The most important thing about pizza making is using a very hot oven - crank it up!

My other two pies in this section call for puff pastry and phyllo (filo) dough. Both are store-bought, and come frozen. They need to be thawed prior to using, but are very easy to work with. Puff pastry you simply unwrap, lightly roll to even the thickness and cut to your desired shape. Phyllo requires no rolling, as it is already paper thin. It can dry out quickly, so cover the stack with a kitchen towel, which will help retain moisture and keep it from breaking. Peel and layer a sheet at a time, coating each with a brush of melted butter. Don't worry if they crack a little; flaws will be indiscernible in the finished product. Phyllo bakes up into the most wonderful crust - crisp and crackling with each bite.

CARAMELIZED ENDIVE TARTE TATIN

Makes 9-inch tart

½ cup water

2 teaspoons cider vinegar

1 teaspoon sugar

1 teaspoon kosher salt

2 tablespoons butter, plus more for buttering your dish

7 heads of endive, cut in half lengthwise

½ cup crumbled semi-dry blue cheese

1 sheet all-butter puff pastry, thawed

The classic tarte tatin is a french dessert; a sweet concoction of apples and delicate pastry. The bottom layer of fruit is cooked in sugar, caramelizing as it bakes, with a flaky layer of puff pastry over top. Out of the oven, it is flipped from the pan so the fruit is on top presenting a dramatic and beautiful - if fairly simple to make - tart. I began dipping into the realm of savory tarte tatin a few years back, and became smitten with this endive version. There is a transformative effect vinegar has on endive, at once bolstering the earthy flavor and cutting through the richness of the dish. Our family is split on using blue cheese or gruyere. Truly both are magical, and if you have a preference go with it - for me, I say blue cheese.

1. Preheat your oven to 400 F. Butter a 9-inch, straight sided pie plate or tart pan. You could also use a cast iron skillet.

2. Combine the water, vinegar, sugar and salt together in a small bowl.

3. Melt the butter over medium heat in a large skillet and when it's hot, add the endive cut side down. Cook until they brown evenly on the bottom, which should take 3-5 minutes, then turn them over and cook for another 2 minutes. Turn down the heat if it begins smoking or looks like they are getting dark too quickly.

4. Pour the water mixture into the pan with the endive. Bring to a simmer, cover and cook for 20 minutes, turning the endive half way through. If there is any liquid left at the end of cooking, remove the lid and turn up the heat to reduce it completely.

5. Place the endive, cut side down, in your prepared baking dish. Put the stem end in the middle, fanning out the endive halves decoratively. They will probably not all fit in one circle, so tuck the remaining endive in the spaces between the fanned out endive in the first circle. Sprinkle the cheese evenly over top.

6. Roll out the puff pastry on a lightly floured board, not too thin, just to even it out, and cut a circle slightly larger than the size of your pan. Drape the pastry over the endive, and tuck in the sides. Cut a few small vents in the pastry with a sharp knife. *The tart can be prepared up to this point, covered and refrigerated for up to 6 hours before baking.*

7. Bake the tart in the preheated oven for 30-40 minutes, until nicely browned. Remove and let cool in the pan for 5 minutes, then invert carefully onto a serving plate. Serve warm.

BAY SCALLOP "CHOWDER" PIZZA

Pizza is kind of my thing, so when I had the privilege of cooking for my father-in-law's 70th birthday, the main course was a no-brainer. I can put just about anything on a pizza, so what did he request? Scallops. Huh. I've topped pizza with many a sea creature, but never a scallop. One of my first rules of pizza making is to ensure the toppings aren't too heavy for the dough. I couldn't see how they could work, until… bay scallops, of course! And where does one often find bay scallops? Chow-dah! All the flavors are here; leeks, bacon (turkey bacon for my in-laws), cream, lemon and wine. Thickened on the stovetop, they create a rich sauce to schmear on the dough. A few torn pieces of fresh mozzarella makes this an unforgettable pizza. Chewy crust, smoky bacon, briny scallops… you are going to just love it. The "sauce" can be prepared hours ahead of time and refrigerated, making it a cinch to put all together at go-time.

Makes a 12-inch pizza

1 tablespoon extra virgin olive oil	½ teaspoon lemon zest (from half of a lemon)
1 strip bacon or turkey bacon	1 teaspoon lemon juice
1 small leek, white part chopped	Freshly cracked black pepper
2 small garlic cloves, grated, crushed or chopped finely	1 teaspoon fresh thyme or oregano leaves
½ cup white wine	2 ounces fresh mozzarella
¼ cup heavy cream	2 tablespoons freshly grated parmigiano
½ teaspoon kosher salt	11 ounce ball of pizza dough, store bought or homemade
6 ounces bay scallops, rinsed and drained	Red pepper flakes for serving, optional

Note: When I haven't been able to find bay scallops, I've used sea scallops, cutting them prior to cooking to the size of bay scallops.

1. If you have a baking stone, place it in the oven on the lowest rack before you turn it on, then preheat your oven to the hottest it will go, around 550 F for most home ovens. If you do not have a pizza stone, you can cook the pizza on a baking sheet lightly dusted with cornmeal or flour. No need to preheat the baking sheet.

2. Pour the olive oil in a medium skillet and place over medium-high heat. Cook the bacon or turkey bacon until crisp. *Turkey bacon will not get super crisp and usually comes precooked, so just cook it until it takes on some color.* Remove, and when cool enough, chop it coarsely. If you use real bacon and have a lot of fat in the skillet, drain off all but about a tablespoon.

3. Add the leek, garlic and salt to the hot skillet, adjusting the heat to medium-low so that it cooks and softens, but isn't browning. Stir occasionally, and after 3 minutes, when the leeks are softened, increase the heat and pour in the wine. Simmer until the wine is mostly reduced, with just a little liquid remaining, which should take about another 3 minutes. Add the cream and bring back to a simmer, and cook for another 2 minutes before adding the scallops. Cook for 1-2 more minutes, stirring, until the cream is quite thick and the scallops are cooked through. Remove from the heat, add the lemon zest, juice, plenty of fresh black pepper and herbs, and stir to combine. Taste for seasoning and add more salt, if needed. *This can be made a few hours ahead of time and refrigerated.*

4. Stretch the dough out on a floured board to roughly a 12-inch circle, leaving a thicker border, about ¾ inch, to form the crust. The interior should be about ¼ inch thick. Make sure the dough has enough flour underneath that it will slide off easily if using a pizza stone. Otherwise, place the dough on your baking sheet. Spread the scallop mixture evenly over the dough, up to the border you've created. Tear pieces of the cheese and scatter it on top, then sprinkle evenly with the parmigiano and the chopped bacon. Bake in the preheated oven until the dough is browned and the pizza is bubbling. Remove, cut into pieces and serve with hot pepper flakes.

BEE STING PIZZA

Makes 12-inch pizza

8-10 thin slices of salami (fewer if they are very large slices)

3 tablespoons tomato sauce

4 ounces fresh mozzarella, torn into pieces

1 jalapeño plus 2 tablespoons white wine vinegar

Kosher salt

Freshly cracked black pepper

11 ounce ball pizza dough, store bought or homemade

1 tablespoon honey

A few leaves of fresh basil

Red pepper flakes for serving

Note: For the best tomato sauce flavor, make your own by emptying a large can of whole tomatoes in a bowl, adding a little olive oil, fresh basil and salt, and crushing together with your hands. This, however, will yield a lot of leftover sauce. Alternatively, you can purchase a small can of premade tomato sauce. Taste to ensure that it is properly seasoned, and if necessary, add salt or pepper before using.

Sweet and spicy is a match made in heaven. This pie is simple, but has such amazing depth. A brush of tomato, thinly sliced salami, a scattering of mozz and chilis - and when it emerges from the piping hot oven, a drizzle of honey. This pizza is the bee's knees.

1. Preheat your oven to the hottest it will go, usually around 550 F for most home ovens. If you have a baking stone, place it in the oven on the lowest rack before you turn it on. If you do not have a pizza stone, you can cook the pizza on a baking sheet, lightly dusted with cornmeal or flour, or lined with parchment.

2. Thinly slice the jalapeño and place in a small bowl or jar. Pour in the vinegar to cover the chilis (use more if needed) and let them sit at room temperature for at least 20 minutes.

3. Stretch the dough out on a floured board to roughly a 12-inch circle, leaving a thicker border, about ¾ inch, to form the crust. The interior should be about ¼ inch thick. Make sure the dough has enough flour underneath that it will slide off easily if using a pizza stone. Otherwise, place the dough on your baking sheet.

4. Spoon the sauce on the dough and spread it out thinly to the border. It's important not to overdo the sauce, it should just be a thin coating. Lay the salami on the sauce, then scatter the cheese. Distribute the chilis over top (leaving the vinegar behind), using more or less depending on your heat preference. Crack black pepper on top, sprinkle with a few pinches of salt, then place in your preheated oven. Cook until golden brown, about 8 minutes if your oven is at 550 F.

5. Remove to a cutting board and drizzle with the honey. Tear the basil over the pizza and serve right away.

HERBY ZUCCHINI PHYLLO PIE

Makes a 9-inch pie

1 package phyllo dough (also called filo), thawed

4 tablespoons melted butter

1 teaspoon extra virgin olive oil

1 ½ pounds zucchini (about 2 medium), sliced as thinly as you can into rounds

2 garlic cloves, sliced

1 teaspoon kosher salt

2 large eggs

⅛ teaspoon caraway seeds

½ cup loosely packed chopped cilantro

2 tablespoons chopped dill

2 tablespoons chopped mint

¾ cup crumbled feta cheese

Freshly cracked black pepper

2 tablespoons pine nuts

Note: Phyllo is sold frozen, and should be thawed before using. You will not use an entire package of dough for this recipe. Check the box for the manufacturer's guidelines on how long it can be stored in the refrigerator, or if you can refreeze it. In either case, make sure to wrap it tightly in plastic wrap so that it does not dry out.

Zucchini are prolific little buggers. When the bounty is on, we're all on the lookout for something new to make. Enter this herby, Greek-inspired zucchini pie. Mint, cilantro and dill bring the zucchini to life, enveloped in a wonderfully simple and buttery phyllo crust. My guess is you will barely notice the caraway seeds as you're eating the pie, however, with their mild anise flavor, they are the unsung hero in this dish. Serve with a green salad as a tasty, light dinner - or alongside other Mediterranean-inspired meze like fattoush, hummus and kabobs. However you enjoy it, this may be the best thing you do with zucchini all season long.

1. Preheat your oven to 375 F.

2. Melt the butter in a large skillet, then pour it into a bowl to use later, leaving roughly a tablespoon in the skillet. Add the olive oil, zucchini, garlic, caraway and ¾ teaspoon salt to the pan and cook over medium-high heat for 5 minutes, stirring frequently and being careful that the garlic doesn't burn. Turn the heat lower if it is browning too quickly. Continue to cook, stirring occasionally, until all of the zucchini is translucent and fully softened, which should take another 15 minutes or so. If there is a significant amount of moisture in the pan at the end of cooking, turn the heat up to cook it off before proceeding. Remove from the heat and let it cool slightly.

3. Crack the eggs into a large bowl and whisk with the remaining ¼ teaspoon salt and add some freshly cracked black pepper. Stir in the herbs and cheese.

4. Use a pastry brush to coat a 9-inch deep pie plate with a little of the melted butter. Unroll the phyllo dough, and keep it covered with a dish towel while you work with it so that it does not dry out. Lay one sheet across the pie plate, there will be a few inches of overhang, then brush it gently or drizzle it with a little of the melted butter. Lay a second sheet perpendicular to the first, and again drizzle with butter. The third sheet lay diagonally, again drizzling with some butter, and the fourth also diagonally, but the other way. Layer two more sheets in the direction in which you began, brushing with butter in between.

5. Mix the zucchini into the egg mixture, then pour that into the phyllo dough. Scatter the pine nuts evenly on the top, then begin folding in the excess dough toward the center. It's okay if it's not perfect, it will bake up into a beautifully flaky mess. Brush a little remaining butter on the top.

6. Bake in your preheated oven for 25-30 minutes, then check for doneness. The top should be browned, and the filling set. Remove and let cool for 5 minutes before cutting, or let sit for up to 90 minutes and serve at room temperature.

CAULIFLOWER CARBONARA

Serves 4

1 medium cauliflower

2 tablespoons extra virgin olive oil

½ teaspoon kosher salt

1 tablespoon fresh rosemary, chopped

2 large garlic cloves, chopped finely

½ cup grated parmigiano reggiano, packed, plus more for passing at the table

2 large eggs

1 teaspoon freshly cracked black pepper

¾ cup frozen peas

12 ounces rigatoni

2 tablespoons kosher salt for the pasta water

Crushed red pepper flakes for serving

Three things are necessary to make this pasta extraordinary. Perhaps most importantly, it begins with a nice roast on the cauliflower, caramelizing the outside and deepening the florets' flavor. Humidity, elevation, and temperature calibration of your oven are factors which will cause the cauliflower to take more or less time. Check it occasionally while roasting, and adjust the temperature for a proper brown. Secondly, make sure you use a good quality grated parmigiano without additives, specifically anti-caking agents, such as cellulose. If you cannot find a good pre-grated parmigiano, buy a hunk and grate it yourself on the small holes of a box grater. Finally, make sure to scoop out and save at least 2 cups of pasta water before you drain the rigatoni. You'd be surprised how quickly the eggs and cheese thicken, and though you may not need all of it, the pasta water is crucial for loosening the sauce. While the pot is on the heat, keep it moving. If you stop stirring, especially soon after the egg mixture is added, the eggs could scramble instead of emulsifying into a thick and creamy sauce.

1. Preheat your oven to 375 F. Cut the core from the cauliflower and discard. Rough chop the cauliflower into 1 ½ to 2-inch chunks and lay on a baking sheet. Drizzle the cauliflower with the olive oil and toss with the salt and rosemary. Bake for 25-30 minutes. The cauliflower should be softened and lightly browned. Stir in the garlic and return to the oven for 5 more minutes. Remove and set aside.

2. While the cauliflower is roasting, bring 5 quarts of water to a boil with the 2 tablespoons of kosher salt. Whisk the eggs in a medium bowl, then whisk the grated cheese and black pepper into the eggs.

3. Cook the pasta according to package directions. You can begin when the cauliflower is close to being done to save time. When the pasta is al dente, scoop out 2 cups of pasta water and add the peas to the pot. Cook pasta and peas for 30 seconds longer, then drain and return them to the pot. Place the pot back onto the stove.

4. Turn the heat to medium. Immediately add the egg and cheese mixture to the pot and stir vigorously using a wooden spoon or silicone spatula. When it begins to thicken, after about 30 seconds to a minute, add ½ cup of the reserved pasta water and stir to incorporate. Stir in the cauliflower. At this point the sauce should be the consistency of a very thick cream, coating the pasta and vegetables. Add more pasta water to loosen the sauce if it is too thick. Don't be afraid of adding too much water, you can always cook it down if that happens. Just be sure to keep stirring so that the sauce stays emulsified instead of scrambling. Taste for seasoning, adding more salt, if needed.

5. Serve right away, passing cheese and pepper flakes at the table.

BRAISED FENNEL & PINE NUT LINGUINE

If I had to name a signature dish, this would be in the running. When I'm out to impress dinner guests, yet keep it simple, this fennel pasta is my go-to. Onions and fennel melt and caramelize into the linguine, with fresh rosemary for spice. The pasta's full potential is achieved with a healthy addition of toasted pine nuts - their tender chew and sweetness plays off the sugar of the caramelized onion and fennel. Don't skip the step of toasting the nuts, as they will not have the same impact without being lightly browned. As with nearly all pasta, success lies in finishing the noodles in the sauce, and adding pasta cooking water to keep the dish loose and luscious. Make certain to stir in the cheese off the heat, otherwise it will seize and become gummy.

Serves 4

¼ cup extra virgin olive oil

1 small sweet onion, sliced

1 teaspoon kosher salt, plus 2 tablespoons for the pasta water

2 medium fennel bulbs, sliced, about 1 ¼ pounds total

4 garlic cloves, chopped finely or crushed

1 tablespoon fresh rosemary, chopped

1 pound linguine

1 cup freshly grated parmigiano reggiano

¼ cup pine nuts, toasted

Freshly cracked black pepper

1. Bring a large pot of water to a boil so it's ready to go when you are. For this amount of pasta I suggest at least 5 quarts. Once it comes to a boil, turn the heat to low just to keep warm while you make the sauce.

2. Prepare to saute the vegetables. Pour the oil in a large stockpot. *I prefer to use a pot for the fennel/onion mixture so that when I add the pasta later there is plenty of room to stir it all together, though if you don't have one, use a skillet that is at least 12 inches with a lid.* Place the pot over medium heat and add the onion and 1 teaspoon of the salt. Cook, stirring occasionally, until softened, about 5 minutes.

3. Add the fennel, garlic and rosemary and saute another 5 minutes, stirring once or twice, until it all begins to soften. If it looks dry, you can add a little bit of water from the pasta pot. Otherwise turn the heat to low, cover with the lid, and cook for 20-30 minutes, stirring 3 or 4 times during cooking. Keep an eye on the moisture and add more water if it seems dry or that it may burn. At the end you want it to all be completely soft, you can't really overcook it, so you can keep it on low heat as the pasta cooks.

4. As the fennel/onion mixture is finishing, begin cooking the pasta. Add two tablespoons of salt to the pasta water and return it to boiling. Cook the linguini until al dente, about 2 minutes shy of being done.

5. Now you can do one of two methods: Either use tongs to transfer the noodles directly into the onions and fennel, keeping the pasta water in the pot, or scoop out about 1 ½ or 2 cups of pasta water, then drain the noodles and add them to the fennel and onions.

6. Stir the noodles and fennel/onions together, adding in ½ cup of reserved pasta water and raising the heat to high. Stir and cook for 2 minutes, tasting a piece of pasta and fennel for seasoning. Add plenty of cracked black pepper, and salt, if needed. Add another ½ cup of water and let it cook down just for a minute, stirring.

7. Remove the pot from the direct heat and add ½ cup of the grated cheese. Stir vigorously so that the cheese emulsifies in the sauce and becomes thick and creamy. Dish out onto individual plates, or one large pasta bowl. Sprinkle with the pine nuts and more cheese, and serve hot.

EGGPLANT "MEATBALLS" WITH SPAGHETTI

Serves 6

FOR THE EGGPLANT:

1 large eggplant (about 1 pound)

1 cup canned chickpeas, rinsed and drained

¾ cup panko bread crumbs

2 tablespoons grated parmigiano

1 large egg plus 1 egg yolk

1 tablespoon chopped parsley

1 small garlic clove, grated or crushed

1 ¼ teaspoons kosher salt

½ teaspoon fennel seed, crushed finely using the back of a chefs knife

FOR THE PASTA:

28 ounce can whole peeled tomatoes

¼ cup fresh basil leaves

2 tablespoons extra virgin olive oil

1 teaspoon kosher salt

1 garlic clove, grated or crushed

1 pound spaghetti

Fresh grated parmigiano for serving

Even though this is a great way to add healthy veggies to your meal, I don't view these as some sort of vegetarian substitute for real meatballs. Eggplant meatballs are a thing unto themselves - and they are a thing of beauty. Don't expect the same flavor or texture as a meatball; they have both feet firmly planted in the world of vedge, but eggplant meatballs are a fun, different, and excellent way to do pasta night. As unique as eggplant is in a meatball, it's the crushed fennel seed that makes them outstanding. It provides a sweet Italian sausage vibe which is such a great pairing with spaghetti and sauce. Cook the pasta in the sauce to finish, infusing the noodles with the tomatoes in the most amazing way.

1. Bring 5 quarts of water to a boil. Turn the heat down and add two tablespoons of kosher salt, then cover and keep warm.

2. Pour the canned tomatoes in a bowl and add the whole basil leaves, salt and olive oil. Crush the tomatoes using your hands, squeezing them until they are mostly broken down with some chunky pieces remaining, squeezing the basil leaves at the same time to impart their flavor into the sauce. Stir in the garlic and set aside.

3. Turn your oven to broil. Prick the eggplant all over with a knife and place on a foil lined baking sheet. Broil, about 6 inches from the heat, until it is beginning to blacken on the top. Carefully turn it to char the other sides. The eggplant is finished when it is very soft and fully charred. Remove from the oven, wrap the foil around it and let it cool. Turn the oven down to 375 F. When the eggplant is cool enough to handle, peel off the skin and put the flesh into a mesh colander that has been set over a bowl, and let the extra liquid drain for 8-10 minutes.

4. Place the beans in a bowl and mash them down using a potato masher (you could also do this in a food processor). The beans should not be totally smooth, but should be mostly broken down with a little texture. Chop the eggplant and add to the bowl with the beans. You can use the potato masher on the eggplant as well if there are any large chunks. Like the beans, it should be mostly broken down with a little texture. Add the remaining ingredients for the meatballs and mix thoroughly.

5. Form the mixture into balls about half the size of a golf ball and place on a baking sheet lined with parchment that has been rubbed with a little olive oil. *You can do this a few hours ahead of time and refrigerate until ready to bake and assemble the pasta.*

6. Return your pot of water to a boil, and at this point put the eggplant

meatballs into the preheated oven. Set a timer for 15 minutes. Next, drop the pasta into the boiling water and cook for 2 minutes shy of the recommended cooking time. Drain the noodles, reserving 1 ½ cups of cooking water.

7. Add the tomatoes and the pasta back into the empty pot, along with ½ cup pasta water and bring them to a simmer. Cook at a brisk simmer for 4 minutes, then check the pasta for doneness and the sauce for seasoning. Add more salt,

if necessary, and if the noodles need longer, continue to simmer until they are done, adding more pasta water as needed.

8. To serve, divide the pasta among individual pasta bowls, or place in one large serving bowl. Top with the eggplant meatballs, a drizzle of olive oil and some fresh basil. Serve hot, passing extra cheese at the table.

SWEET POTATO PIEROGI

Makes 36 dumplings

FOR THE DOUGH:

3 cups (360 grams) all-purpose flour

1 large egg

1 cup sour cream

¼ cup milk

½ teaspoon kosher salt

FOR THE FILLING:

1 large sweet potato (about 1 pound), peeled and cut into ½" cubes

⅛ teaspoon kosher salt

⅛ teaspoon freshly grated nutmeg

Freshly cracked black pepper

TO FINISH:

6 tablespoons unsalted butter

1 medium onion, chopped

1 teaspoon chopped rosemary, or use thyme or sage

½ teaspoon kosher salt

Pih-ROH-hee, that's how my grandma pronounced it. Her parents emigrated from Slovakia, and as a kid we enjoyed all sorts of traditional dishes, which to me sounded so funny at the time. Halloupki, bobalki, pagach - but one of my favorites has always been pirohy (Slovak for the more widely known, pierogi). She made them with lots and lots of browned onions and butter, which are present here; my twist is a sweet potato filling spiked with fresh nutmeg in place of the traditional white potato. This is a great stuffed pasta to try out if you are a novice - the dough is a breeze to work with and the filling is a cinch to bring together. These freeze beautifully, so go on and make a big batch like my grandmother would!

1. Whisk the egg, sour cream, milk and salt in the bowl of a stand mixer. Add the flour and using the dough hook, mix on low speed until the dough comes together. If it seems dry, add a bit more milk. If it seems too sticky, add more flour. Knead 3-4 minutes, then cover with plastic wrap and let it rest for 20 minutes at room temperature, or a few hours in the refrigerator. You could also mix this by hand.

2. While the dough rests, place the sweet potatoes and plenty of water in a medium saucepan and bring to a simmer. Cook for 15 minutes or so until the potatoes are fork tender. The exact time will depend on the type of sweet potato you have. Make sure that a fork easily pierces the potatoes.

3. Now, get your onions going. Melt the butter over medium heat in a large skillet. Add the onion, herbs and ½ teaspoon salt. Cook over medium heat for 8-10 minutes, stirring occasionally, then turn the heat to low and cover partially. Let them keep cooking over the lowest heat while you assemble the pierogi. Check on them every once and a while and give them a stir. You can add some water if they seem dry.

4. Bring a large pot of water to a simmer (about 5 quarts), season with a tablespoon of salt and then turn down and keep warm over low heat.

5. Drain the potatoes well, and mash them with a potato masher until there are no lumps. Season with plenty of freshly cracked black pepper, the nutmeg and the ⅛ teaspoon salt.

6. Roll the dough out on a floured surface to ⅛ inch thick. Use a 3-inch round cookie or biscuit cutter to cut out as many rounds as you can. Gather the scraps and wrap them up again while you make the first batch.

7. Fill each round with about a tablespoon of sweet potato. Brush the edges with a little water, then fold in half and crimp the edges to seal. Place on a floured baking sheet and continue with the rest. Reroll any dough and repeat the process until it is all used.

8. To cook the pierogi, return the pot of water to a boil and drop them in carefully. Cook for 4 minutes (6-8 if cooking frozen), then remove with a slotted spoon to the skillet with the onions. Raise the heat and cook them in the onions and butter for a minute or two until they are coated with the butter. If they look too dry, add a little cooking water from the pot to loosen. Serve warm.

To make the pierogi ahead and freeze, skip steps 3 and 4. After step 7, lay them on a parchment lined sheet pan and place in the freezer. Once frozen, transfer to a plastic bag and freeze for up to a month.

FETTUCCINE WITH SEARED CALAMARI & PAN ROASTED TOMATOES

Serves 4

FOR THE BASIL SAUCE:

2 tablespoons lemon juice

2 garlic cloves, chopped finely or grated

2 tablespoons chopped fresh basil

½ teaspoon freshly cracked black pepper

⅛ teaspoon kosher salt

1 tablespoon extra virgin olive oil

TO MAKE THE PASTA:

4 tablespoons extra virgin olive oil, plus more for finishing the dish

1 pound raw squid, cleaned and cut into rings

1 pound grape or cherry tomatoes, large ones halved

1 small white onion, peeled, halved and sliced thinly

1 teaspoon kosher salt, plus 2 tablespoons for the pasta water

12 ounces fettuccine

4 cups loosely packed arugula (about 3 ounces)

Red pepper flakes and grated parmigiano for serving

Note: Use either fresh or frozen (and thawed) squid. Check with the fishmonger or packaging that it is cleaned to make it easier to prep at home. You may use tubes only, or a combination of tubes and tentacles.

Calamari (squid) is a very easy to cook, inexpensive and flavorful seafood. The trick to getting the texture just right is to either cook it *long and low* or *fast and hot*. Here I do the latter, with a quick sear to seal in the juices, then marinate it in a lemony basil sauce, adding it back into the pasta at the end. As the cooked squid bathes in the sauce, it absorbs the bright and fresh flavors of citrus and herbs. This is a weeknight pasta dinner that will taste like a night out at an Italian trattoria!

1. Begin by bringing a large pot with 5 quarts of water to a boil. Turn the heat to low and add two tablespoons of kosher salt, then put the lid on and keep warm.

2. Combine all the ingredients for the basil sauce in a medium bowl.

3. Pour 2 tablespoons of the olive oil in a large skillet and warm over high heat. Add the squid and ½ teaspoon salt and cook, stirring the entire time, for 1-2 minutes. The squid will cook quickly, and will become rubbery if you leave it in too long. They are done when they firm up, shrinking just slightly in size. Remove with a slotted spoon and place in the bowl with the basil sauce, stirring to coat.

4. Pour the other tablespoon of olive oil into the pan and immediately add the tomatoes and onions. Season with the other ½ teaspoon salt, give it a stir and after a minute put the lid on and turn the heat to medium. Shake the pan a few times, with the lid on, then after 3 minutes check the tomatoes. Most of them should be burst open, with some whole tomatoes remaining. Give them a stir, replace the lid and cook for another few minutes. Once the tomatoes look mostly broken down and the onions are soft, remove the lid and keep warm over low heat.

5. Return the water in the pot to a boil and add the pasta. When it has two minutes left of cooking time, add the arugula to the pan with the tomatoes, give it a stir and add some freshly cracked black pepper, replacing the lid.

6. Scoop out about a cup of cooking water before you drain the pasta, or use tongs to transfer the fettucini directly from the water to the pan with the tomatoes and arugula retaining the cooking water. Stir pasta into the tomato/arugula mixture, adding a half cup of the pasta water. Cook and let the flavors meld together for a minute. Add a little more pasta water if it looks like it needs to be loosened. Add the cooked squid and its marinade to the pasta, and stir with tongs to combine. Taste for seasoning, adding more salt and pepper, if needed.

7. To serve, dish out into pasta bowls or a large serving bowl, passing grated cheese and pepper flakes at the table.

FOOLPROOF CACIO E PEPE

Serves 4

4 tablespoons unsalted butter at room temperature

½ cup pecorino romano, grated on the fine holes of a box grater

¼ cup parmigiano reggiano, grated on the fine holes of a box grater

1 ½ teaspoons freshly cracked black pepper

½ teaspoon kosher salt plus 2 tablespoons for the pasta water

12 ounces bucatini, or other pasta such as tagliatelle

Fresh parmigiano for serving

The classic Roman pasta dish has taken hold in today's culinary scene; it's become so trendy that chefs are doing riffs like "cacio e pepe" pizza, risotto, cheese puffs and so on. Of course there's a reason for the craze - it's dang good! The traditional version also happens to be fairly difficult to execute properly, despite its simple ingredients. If you're not careful, the cheese can seize, creating a gummy mess instead of a beautiful thick sauce. My foolproof technique utilizes a compound butter that is tossed with the cooked pasta off the heat. The butter is simple to make and can be done ahead and refrigerated for a few days or frozen for up to a month.

1. Begin by bringing a large pot with 5 quarts of water to a boil. Turn the heat to low and add two tablespoons of the kosher salt, then put the lid on and keep warm.

2. Place the cheeses, black pepper and soft butter in a mini food processor and blend together. If you do not have a processor, you can mash it all together in a bowl, making sure it is all thoroughly combined. Place the butter mixture in a large serving bowl.

3. Bring the water back to a boil and add the pasta. Cook until al dente, then drain the pasta, reserving ½ cup pasta water. Immediately pour the drained pasta into the butter and stir to combine. Add pasta water, ¼ cup to begin with, and stir well. If it looks too dry, add a little more water and stir again. Taste for seasoning and add more salt, if necessary. Serve with the grated parmigiano.

CREAMY BAKED ORECCHIETTE & JERUSALEM ARTICHOKES

Serves 4

12 ounces orecchiette

2 tablespoons plus 2 teaspoons kosher salt, divided use

1 ½ pounds Jerusalem artichokes (also called sunchokes)

4 large garlic cloves, peeled and sliced

1 tablespoon fresh thyme

1 ½ cups chicken broth or vegetable broth

¾ cup half and half

Freshly cracked black pepper

1 cup grated fontina cheese (about 3 ounces)

2 cups roughly torn sourdough bread

¼ cup hazelnuts, toasted and skins rubbed off

2 tablespoons butter, plus more for buttering your dish

½ teaspoon kosher salt

½ cup grated parmigiano cheese, plus more for passing at the table

Note: When Jerusalem artichokes are very fresh, you don't need to peel them, just give them a little scrub with a vegetable brush and trim any dark spots. If the peel looks thick, or they are particularly dirty, trim with a paring knife or vegetable peeler.

Jerusalem artichokes are not yet mainstream... and that's a shame! Also known as sunchokes, they may be found in many markets through fall and winter. Roasting sunchokes simply with olive oil and salt is an easy and delicious way to prepare them as a veggie side, but one of the best ways to enjoy them is in a creamy pasta dish. Less starchy than a potato, with a subtle sweetness, they soak up the flavors of the sauce and provide a textural compliment to the pasta. Hazelnuts make a perfect pairing with Jerusalem artichokes; their distinctive aroma and earthy flavor is a match made in heaven.

1. Preheat your oven to 375 F. Butter a 7 x 11-inch baking dish.

2. Trim the Jerusalem artichokes and peel them if the skin is thick or particularly dirty. Cut the large ones in half lengthwise, and slice as thinly as possible, ⅛ inch or less. Pour the broth, half and half and ½ teaspoon salt in the pot and bring to a simmer. Add the Jerusalem artichokes, garlic and thyme and cook at a simmer for 15-20 minutes, until the sunchokes are soft. The exact amount of time will depend on how thinly you slice them, so taste to see when they are tender.

3. While the sunchokes are cooking, bring a large stockpot of water to a boil and season with two tablespoons of salt for 5 quarts of water. Add the pasta and cook until al dente.

4. Drain the pasta, and add it to the pot with the sunchokes along with another teaspoon of salt, season with freshly cracked black pepper and stir well. Taste the liquid, and add more salt if it's needed. Stir in the shredded cheese, then pour into the prepared baking dish.

5. Chop the hazelnuts finely on a cutting board using a chef's knife, then place the bread on top of them and chop it all together, so you end up with large chunky bread crumbs. Sprinkle the salt over top, then tear off pieces of the soft butter and scatter it over top. Use your hands to mush it all together. Sprinkle the cheese over the bread and mix together, then scatter it over the pasta. *At this point you could refrigerate the pasta for a few hours before baking.*

6. Bake in the preheated oven for 15-20 minutes, until bubbling and the bread crumbs are toasty. Serve warm, passing more cheese at the table.

PROTEIN

Whether you're hosting a dinner party, crave a supremely tasty midweek meal, a Sunday family supper or something fun to throw on the grill, my protein-focused mains bring the zest!

Chicken pot pie gets amped up with Moroccan flavors. Turkey meatballs are bathed in a deliciously sticky orange-pomegranate glaze. Shrimp are basted in a homemade barbecue sauce made with fresh peaches, chipotle and bourbon. And simple cod gets boosted by a guajillo chili and roasted tomato sauce.

These dishes bring bold, elevated flavor to your dinner table.

Cooking times are guidelines when it comes to meat and seafood. Many variables are involved, such as the type of fish you purchase and its thickness, the size of your shrimp, or weight of your whole chicken.

Use your senses. How does it look? How does it feel? Is it firm when you press on the meat, or does it still have some give? A thermometer can come in handy if you have one, especially for whole roasted chicken. Avoid cutting into meat before it is finished, or has time to rest, as this releases its juices, causing it to become dry.

CRISPY COCONUT FISH WITH SESAME BROCCOLI & UDON NOODLES

Pan fried fish fillets get punched up with a toasted coconut crust and placed atop citrusy udon noodles. Bathed in a simple ponzu sauce, and flecked with fresh herbs and roasted broccoli, this one-dish dinner is addictive in every way... with crunchy fish, garlicky broccoli & zippy noodles. It's a meal the whole family will love.

Serves 4

FOR THE FISH:

1 ¼ pounds firm white fish, such as haddock, cod or halibut, cut into 8 even pieces and patted dry

2 large eggs

1 teaspoon kosher salt

½ cup flour

½ cup panko bread crumbs

¾ cup toasted coconut flakes

6 tablespoons sesame oil, non-toasted

FOR THE SAUCE:

¼ cup fresh grapefruit juice

3 tablespoons rice wine vinegar

2 tablespoons orange juice

2 tablespoons mirin

2 tablespoons soy sauce

1 teaspoon grated fresh ginger

1 tablespoon dark brown sugar

½ teaspoon kosher salt

FOR THE NOODLES AND BROCCOLI:

10 ounces udon noodles

1 head broccoli

2 tablespoons sesame oil, non-toasted

2 large garlic cloves, chopped

1 teaspoon kosher salt

½ cup chopped fresh basil, mint and cilantro combined

¼ cup unsalted shelled sunflower seeds

1. Preheat your oven to 375 F. Cut the florets from the head of broccoli and cut them into 1-inch pieces. Cut the stem of the broccoli crosswise into thin slices, stopping when the stem becomes woody at the bottom and discard that portion. Toss the broccoli florets and sliced stem with the 2 tablespoons of sesame oil and 1 teaspoon salt and place in a roasting dish or sheet pan. Cook for 20 minutes, until softened and browned. If it is not browning, turn on your broiler for 5-10 minutes until they become slightly charred. Remove from the oven and toss with the garlic.

2. While the broccoli is roasting, prep the rest of the dish. Prepare the sauce by combining all of the ingredients in a bowl. *This can be made a day ahead and refrigerated.*

3. Cook the noodles according to package directions, then rinse and drain very well and return to the pot. Toss ¾ of the sauce with the noodles, and replace the lid to keep warm.

4. Combine the flour and salt in one bowl, and the panko and coconut in a separate large shallow bowl. Use your hands to break up the coconut flakes into small pieces and mix them with the breadcrumbs. Beat the eggs in a third bowl. Dredge the fish in the flour, then dip it in the eggs, and then coat the pieces generously with the bread crumbs and coconut mixture.

5. Heat a large skillet over high heat. Add the 6 tablespoons of sesame oil, then carefully lay the fish in the pan. When it is nicely browned on the bottom, flip and cook the other side. Adjust the heat if the oil is smoking, and cook the fish in batches if it all won't fit without crowding. The exact amount of time it will take to cook depends on the variety and thickness of your fish.

6. Toss the broccoli with the noodles and transfer to a serving bowl. Toss with most of the herbs, leaving a tablespoon or two to sprinkle on the top as garnish.

7. When the fish is cooked through, transfer it to the bowl with the noodles and sprinkle with the sunflower seeds and remaining herbs. Pass the last bit of sauce at the table for whomever would like more.

SEARED SCALLOPS WITH BASIL MINT PESTO & LEMONY ARTICHOKE RISOTTO

Risottos don't have to be laborious, or tricky, or overly rich. A bit of stirring is required, but the notion that one must stand in front of the pot for 30 minutes to achieve great risotto is incorrect. Here, a few vigorous stirs with a wooden spoon at the right time will do the trick. Topped with quickly seared scallops, and served with an herby almond and fresh mint pesto, this Italian-inspired dinner is restaurant worthy, yet so easy to make at home.

Serves 4

FOR THE RISOTTO:

1 tablespoon extra virgin olive oil

½ tablespoon unsalted butter

½ large onion, chopped

2 large garlic cloves, chopped

3-4 cups low-sodium chicken broth

1 lemon

1 cup arborio rice

½ teaspoon kosher salt

14 ounce can artichokes in water, drained and halved

¼ cup grated parmigiano

Freshly cracked black pepper

FOR THE PESTO:

½ cup basil leaves

¼ cup mint leaves

2 garlic cloves

2 tablespoons raw unsalted almonds

1 tablespoon juice from the lemon

½ teaspoon kosher salt

2 tablespoons extra virgin olive oil

FOR THE SCALLOPS:

12 fresh sea scallops

2 tablespoons unsalted butter

Salt and pepper

1. Begin by making the risotto. Warm the oil and butter in a medium saucepan. Add the onion and a pinch of salt and cook over medium heat until softened, about 8 minutes. Add the garlic, ½ teaspoon of salt and the rice and cook, stirring, for 1-2 minutes. Pour in two cups of the broth and bring to a simmer. Use a vegetable peeler to get two wide and long strips of peel from the lemon and drop them in the pot. Cover and reduce the heat to low.

2. While the rice is cooking, make the pesto. Toast the almonds in a toaster oven or dry skillet, then place them in a small bowl and pour boiling water over them to cover. Let them sit for 5-10 minutes, then slip the skins off and discard the water. Place the almonds in a mini food processor with the garlic and blend until the almonds are ground. Place all of the remaining ingredients in the processor except the oil and blend for 30 seconds, scraping down the sides once or twice. Add the oil, then blend again until you have a smooth puree. Transfer to a small bowl.

3. Check on the rice after 10 minutes. Vigorously stir it for about 30 seconds, and add another cup of broth. Return the lid and continue to cook for another 10 minutes, afterwhich stir vigorously for another 30 seconds and check for doneness at this point. If the rice needs to cook longer, add another half cup of broth and return the lid.

4. When the rice is finished cooking, give it another good stir, adding the remaining ½ cup of broth if it is getting too thick. Remove the lemon peels, stir in the artichoke hearts and taste for seasoning. Add more salt, if needed, and plenty of black pepper. Cover and keep warm while you cook the scallops.

5. Place a large skillet over high heat and add the butter. Season the scallops with salt and pepper on both sides, then place in the hot skillet. Cook for about 90 seconds per side. Adjust the heat if the pan is too hot and the butter is burning. It is okay if it browns, but you don't want it to blacken.

6. To serve, stir two tablespoons of the cheese into the risotto off the heat, then dish out onto individual plates. Top each plate with 3 scallops, and dollop the scallops evenly with the pesto. Serve right away, passing more cheese at the table.

ORANGE MISO ROASTED SALMON & BLISTERED SESAME GREEN BEANS

Serves 4

FOR THE FISH:

1 ½ pounds of salmon, cut into 4 portions

3 tablespoons white miso

2 tablespoons dark brown sugar

1 ½ teaspoons grated fresh ginger

1 ½ teaspoons orange zest

1 ½ tablespoons juice from the orange

½ teaspoon kosher salt

FOR THE BEANS:

12 ounces green beans, trimmed

2 tablespoons sesame oil, non-toasted

4 garlic cloves, thinly sliced

¼ teaspoon kosher salt

Juice from half of the orange (2-ish tablespoons)

2 tablespoons sesame seeds

2 teaspoons oyster sauce

OPTIONAL FOR SERVING:

Cooked rice or Asian noodles

Miso, ginger and orange are a magical combination of flavors when roasted atop flaky, moist salmon. Miso, a fermented soy paste, adds a rich umami element without being heavy. Crunchy sesame green beans are a humble, yet worthy accompaniment to the king of fish. Round out the dish with soba noodles tossed with a drizzle of hot chili oil, or with simple, steamed rice.

1. Preheat your oven to 400 F.

2. Rinse the salmon and pat dry, then place in a foil lined baking pan or baking sheet. If your salmon is skinless, oil the bottom of the salmon to prevent sticking. Mix together the remaining ingredients for the salmon in a small bowl, then spread the miso mixture evenly over the salmon. Set aside while you cook the beans.

3. Heat a 12-inch cast iron skillet or other large skillet over high heat. It's best not to use a non-stick skillet for this, as the beans will not blister properly. Add the sesame oil to the pan and fry the garlic slices until light brown, which should take 1-2 minutes. Remove with a slotted spoon to a small dish. Immediately add the beans and salt to the pan, which should be very hot. Let them cook, without stirring, for 1-2 minutes. Adjust the heat if it is smoking too much, stir the beans and continue to cook. Keep cooking and stirring occasionally until the green beans are cooked and have taken on some color. It will probably take another 5-7 minutes. Add the orange juice, oyster sauce and sesame seeds and stir until the sauce thickens. It shouldn't take too long, then turn off the heat.

4. Place the salmon in the hot oven and cook for 10 minutes. The amount of time your salmon takes to cook depends on the type of fish you buy, and also if you prefer it pink in the middle or cooked through. A sockeye or coho will take less time than a thicker king or Atlantic salmon. When it feels almost done, turn on your broiler and broil the fish to finish cooking and lightly brown the miso topping.

5. If you've cooked your beans in cast iron, they are probably still warm enough. Otherwise gently rewarm them before serving with the salmon, either on a large platter or individual plates. Sprinkle the beans with the garlic chips before serving.

COD STEWED WITH ROASTED TOMATOES, CHILIS & OLIVES

Serves 4 – *enjoy with Simple Focaccia Bread*

6 Roma tomatoes

5 garlic cloves, peel left on

½ teaspoon ground ginger

2 teaspoons coconut sugar or brown sugar

1 ½ teaspoon kosher salt

1 teaspoon extra virgin olive oil, plus more for drizzling at the end

2 medium guajillo chilis, stems removed, split open and seeds removed

1 teaspoon cumin seeds

1 tablespoon red wine vinegar

2 teaspoons honey

1 cup kalamata olives

3 tablespoons chopped fresh basil

Freshly cracked black pepper

1 ½ pounds cod, cut into 1" pieces

FOR SERVING:

Grated parmigiano and red pepper flakes

Warm focaccia or rustic Italian bread

Note: If dried chilis are too brittle to stem and seed, toast them whole in the skillet for 20-30 seconds per side. Once warmed, they will be easier to open, seed and stem.

Dried chilis are a fantastic way to add a bit of zesty to your cooking. Nowadays, most grocery stores stock a variety. Guajillos are one of the mildest, and add great flavor with a modest heat. Sometimes they are labeled as "cascavel" chilis, not to be confused with "cascabel" chilies, which are round in shape and much spicier. If you cannot find guajillo, substitute one ancho chili. I prefer to use non-pitted olives in this stew, as they impart additional flavor, but if you are concerned with accidentally chomping down on a pit, use pitted. I've included a bonus recipe - my favorite focaccia bread - which goes great with this stew, however, an artisan Italian bread will do if you're not up for baking.

1. Turn the oven to broil and position a rack 6 inches from the heat. Line a pie plate or small baking dish with foil.

2. Core the tomatoes, cut in half lengthwise and place in the dish, skin side down. Sprinkle with the ginger, sugar and a pinch of salt per tomato, then drizzle the teaspoon of olive oil over the tomatoes. Place the unpeeled garlic in the dish, then place the dish under the broiler. Turn the garlic after 3 minutes, then remove it after 5 so that it doesn't burn. Continue to roast the tomatoes until they start to char a bit, but don't let them burn. It should take 15-20 minutes. Remove from the oven and let cool slightly.

3. Place a small skillet over medium-low heat. Toast the cumin seed for a minute or two, then remove from the pan. You can place them directly in your blender jar. Put the chilis in the hot skillet and dry toast them, being careful not to let them burn. Turn them a few times, toasting the skin side and the interior. They should be finished in about 2 minutes. Place in a bowl and cover with warm water until they are softened, about 5 minutes.

4. Remove the chilis from the water and place in the blender. Slip the skins off the tomatoes and the garlic and also add to the blender, along with the honey and teaspoon of salt. Blend for 1-2 minutes until totally smooth.

5. Pour the sauce into a saucepan and add the vinegar, olives and basil. Bring to a simmer and let it cook gently for 5 minutes. Add the fish and cook for another 5 minutes, stirring once or twice, and being careful not to break it up too much. The fish should be cooked through after 5 minutes, but cook longer if it's not. Taste for seasoning, and add more salt, if needed. Add plenty of freshly cracked black pepper, then spoon into bowls.

6. Serve with a drizzle of extra virgin olive oil, passing grated parmigiano, a bowl of pepper flakes and fresh bread at the table.

SIMPLE FOCACCIA BREAD

Makes a 9-inch square loaf

3 cups (360 grams) all-purpose flour

1 ¼ teaspoons kosher salt

1 package active dry yeast (2 ½ teaspoons)

2 teaspoons sugar

5 tablespoons extra virgin olive oil

Flaky salt for sprinkling on the top

Optional chopped rosemary or sliced black olives for topping

The key to really great focaccia bread is really good olive oil, and lots of it. Don't skimp, it makes all the difference.

1. Combine the flour and salt in the bowl of a stand mixer fitted with the dough hook.

2. Dissolve the sugar and yeast in 1 cup plus 2 tablespoons of warm water in a small bowl. Let it sit for 5-10 minutes until foamy, then add one tablespoon of olive oil.

3. Turn the mixer on low and pour yeast mixture into the bowl with the flour and salt. Add a little more water if there is still dry flour on the bottom of the bowl. Knead for 5 minutes then cover with plastic wrap and let it rise for 1 hour. You can also do all of this by hand, mixing the flour and liquid together in a bowl and then kneading it for 8-10 minutes on a floured board.

4. After an hour, punch down the dough, cover and let rise again for another 30 minutes.

5. Pour 3 tablespoons of the olive oil in a 9 x 9-inch metal baking pan. Place the dough into the pan (I use my dough scraper to get it out of the bowl, but hands or a spatula work fine if you don't have one). Use your hands to press it into the shape of the pan. Turn the dough over so that it is all coated with the oil. It will seem like a lot of oil, but that is the point. Use your fingertips to push the dough to the edges, which will make dimples all over the top to create the classic focaccia look, then cover the pan with plastic wrap.

6. Let the dough rise again for 30 minutes, or refrigerate for up to 4 hours. *Let it sit on the counter for 30-40 minutes before baking if it has been refrigerated.* Preheat your oven to 400 F while the dough is resting.

7. Remove the plastic wrap, drizzle with the last tablespoon of olive oil, and sprinkle the dough with flaky salt, and chopped rosemary and olives, if using. Bake for 15-20 minutes until golden brown.

8. Remove from the oven, let cool for at least 10 minutes in the pan, then remove to a cutting board and cut into squares with a serrated knife.

GRILLED SHRIMP BASTED WITH PEACH BOURBON BBQ SAUCE

Serves 6

1 tablespoon extra virgin olive oil

1 medium shallot, chopped

1 garlic clove, chopped

1 Roma tomato, chopped

1 small chipotle chili from a can of chipotles in adobo, seeded and chopped

1 teaspoon sauce from the can of chipotles

½ teaspoon dried mustard powder

⅛ teaspoon caraway seeds

1 cup sliced peaches

¼ cup bourbon

¼ cup pure maple syrup

1 teaspoon kosher salt

1 teaspoon freshly cracked black pepper

1 tablespoon soy sauce

2 pounds large peeled shrimp

Wooden skewers

A sweet, sticky, summer-inspired barbecue sauce for skewered shrimp, fortified with plenty of bourbon, a kick from chipotles, and of course, the star of the show, ripe, juicy peaches. No grill? No problem. Sear off the shrimp in a hot skillet. Skewering is optional. Good go-withs? A pan of moist, jalapeño-studded cornbread, and a crisp, cabbage slaw (I've got great recipes for both on my blog:) If you want a more intense heat, use two chipotles and don't seed them.

1. Warm the oil in a small saucepan and saute the shallot and garlic over medium heat with a half teaspoon of the salt. Cook for 2-3 minutes, then add the tomato, chipotle and sauce, mustard powder and caraway seeds. Cook for 3-4 minutes, stirring once or twice. Add the peaches, bourbon and maple syrup and cook for another 5 minutes.

2. Transfer the mixture to a blender or food processor and blend until completely smooth, at least 30 seconds. Be careful when blending hot liquids. Cover the blender jar with a dish towel and keep a firm hand on it as the heat can cause the top to pop off.

3. Return the sauce to the pot, add the soy sauce and cook for another 10 minutes over medium-low heat, partially covered to avoid splatters. Add the black pepper and remove from the heat. Let it cool.

4. Pour half of the sauce over the shrimp in a large bowl. Let them marinate for 20 minutes. Set aside the remaining sauce for serving.

5. Use two skewers to pierce each shrimp, skewering about 5 shrimp per set of parallel skewers, or however many fit comfortably based on your skewer size. *The point of using two skewers instead of one is so that the shrimp can't spin on the skewer, which allows you to flip them over easily on the grill.*

6. Heat your grill to medium-high. Grill the shrimp for 1-2 minutes per side, until they are cooked through but not over done. The exact amount of time depends on how large your shrimp are. After you flip them once, brush with a little more sauce. Discard any leftover marinade from the raw shrimp.

7. Remove to a serving platter and serve with the remaining sauce that was set aside.

INDIAN BUTTER TOFU WITH SQUASH & CHICKPEAS

Serves 6

3 tablespoons butter, or ghee

1 small onion, chopped finely

1 serrano chili, seeded and chopped, or use ½ Anaheim chili for less heat

4 large garlic cloves, grated or chopped finely

2 teaspoons freshly grated ginger

2 teaspoons ground cumin

2 teaspoons garam masala

2 teaspoons fresh grated turmeric, or use 1 teaspoon ground turmeric

½ teaspoon ground coriander

1 ½ teaspoons kosher salt

1 large cinnamon stick

8 ounce can tomato sauce

1 cup low-sodium chicken broth or water

1 can reduced-fat coconut milk

1 small butternut squash (about 3 cups), peeled, seeded and cut into ½" cubes

1 can chickpeas, drained

1 pound extra firm tofu, cut into ¾" cubes

Juice from ½ lemon

¼ cup chopped cilantro

TO SERVE:

Cooked rice and/or naan

2 tablespoons cashews, optional

A few spices, a can of coconut milk, tomato sauce and chickpeas, and in about 30 minutes it'll taste like you just traveled halfway around the world. If you can get your hands on fresh turmeric, it's a lovely ingredient, creating that unmistakable curry-like flavor, and distinctive yellow hue. In reading through the recipe you might ask why to add the cumin and garam masala in two additions? Over the years in making this dish, I've always found myself wanting more seasoning when it was time to serve, so I would stir in more cumin and garam masala to finish. While testing and perfecting this recipe, I realized that rather than increasing the measurements up front, that this is the way it should be made - the addition at the end bumps up the flavors and completes the dish. If making this in a warmer season, sweet potato or cauliflower could be substituted for butternut squash.

1. First, get your seasonings organized in a pinch bowl so they are ready to go. Place the garlic, ginger, 1 teaspoon of the cumin and 1 teaspoon of the garam masala, all of the turmeric, 1 teaspoon salt, the coriander, and the cinnamon stick in the bowl.

2. Melt the butter or ghee in a large stock pot. Saute the onion with a pinch of salt over medium heat until softened, about 8 minutes. Add the chili pepper and cook for one more minute before adding in the contents of your pinch bowl. Cook, stirring, for another minute, until the spices begin to stick to the bottom of the pan.

3. Add the tomato sauce, scraping up any stuck spices from the bottom of the pot, and cook for 2 minutes until it begins to thicken. Add the broth and squash and bring to a simmer. Make sure that the squash is submerged in the liquid, adding more if needed to cover. Cook, partially covered, until the squash is just beginning to become tender, about 10 minutes.

4. Stir in the tofu, coconut milk and chickpeas and return to a simmer. Partially cover the pot and let it cook for another 10 minutes, before adding the remaining cumin and garam masala.

5. Taste for seasoning and add more salt, if needed. Depending on the sweetness of the tomato sauce that is used, I sometimes add a teaspoon of sugar at this point if I determine that it will benefit from additional sweetness.

6. Just before serving, stir in the cilantro and about a tablespoon of lemon juice. Serve with cooked rice or warm naan, sprinkling with cashews.

PORCINI PESTO POLENTA WITH SAUSAGE & LEEKS

Dried mushrooms are a worthy asset for every pantry, effortlessly adding rich and deep flavor to soups, stews and pastas. Here, they are not rehydrated, but instead ground to a powder and blended with garlic, pine nuts and herbs to create a thick and flavorful pesto. Stirred into a hot pot of creamy polenta makes a fantastic dish on its own - but topped with savory sausage and leeks, and you have a knockout dinner. You may have a little pesto left over, which will keep in the refrigerator for at least a week. It can add flavor to vegetable soups, be tossed with pasta or smeared on sandwiches.

Serves 6

FOR THE MUSHROOM PESTO:

½ ounce dried porcini mushrooms

2 garlic cloves, grated or crushed

2 tablespoons toasted pine nuts

1 teaspoon chopped fresh rosemary

2 tablespoons chopped parsley

¼ cup grated parmigiano

½ teaspoon kosher salt

½ teaspoon freshly cracked black pepper

2 tablespoons extra virgin olive oil

FOR THE POLENTA AND SAUSAGE:

1 ¼ cups fine dry polenta, not the kind sold in a tube

4-5 cups water

1 teaspoon kosher salt

1 tablespoon extra virgin olive oil

1 large leek, chopped (you may substitute a small, sweet onion, sliced)

1 ½ pounds sweet Italian sausage (chicken or pork)

Freshly cracked black pepper

Grated parmigiano and red pepper flake for passing at the table

1. For the pesto, place the dried mushrooms in a mini food processor and blend until they are a powder. Add the garlic, pine nuts, herbs, cheese, salt and pepper and blend again, scraping the sides and making sure everything is finely ground. Pour in the oil and blend to incorporate. Remove to a small bowl and set aside. Pesto can be made a few hours ahead.

2. Bring 4 cups of water and the 1 teaspoon of salt to a boil in a large saucepan. While whisking, pour in the polenta, and continue whisking continuously until it returns to a simmer. Reduce the heat, cover and cook for 30 minutes, stirring every 8-10 minutes and checking the liquid. You may need to add up to a cup more during the cooking process depending on the type of polenta you are using and how much liquid it absorbs.

3. While the polenta cooks, warm the olive oil in a medium skillet and cook the leeks over medium heat.

When they are softened, after about 5 minutes, remove the sausage from its casing and add to the pan. You may need a little more oil if you are using a chicken sausage, less if using a fattier pork sausage. Cook over medium heat, breaking the sausage up with a spoon, until it is cooked through. Add freshly cracked black pepper to taste, and check the seasoning. If needed, season the meat and leeks with some salt. Keep warm over low heat while the polenta finishes cooking.

4. Once the polenta is fully cooked, add ¾ of the mushroom pesto and stir to combine well. The polenta should be like a thick porridge. Add a little more water if it is too thick. Taste for seasoning, adding more pesto if you would like more of the pesto flavor, and more salt and pepper, if needed.

5. To serve, spoon the polenta into individual bowls and top with equal amounts of sausage and leeks. Pass extra cheese and pepper flakes at the table.

If you do not use all of the pesto, leftovers can be used for pasta, smeared on a sandwich, or tossed with roasted potatoes or other vegetables.

MOROCCAN SPICED CHICKEN POT PIE

Serves 6

2 tablespoons unsalted butter

1 medium onion, chopped

4 garlic cloves, minced

½ teaspoon fresh ginger, grated

2 teaspoons sweet paprika

1 ½ teaspoons ground cinnamon

1 teaspoon ground turmeric

1 teaspoon dried mint, or substitute dried oregano

1 teaspoon kosher salt

Freshly cracked black pepper

½ cup dried green lentils

2 cups low-sodium chicken broth

2 cups sweet potato, cut into ½ inch cubes

2 cups shredded rotisserie chicken

1 package all butter puff pastry, thawed

This Moroccan twist transforms typical pot pie from traditional comfort food to a new, bold and exciting dish. Nevermind the panoply of zesty spices - garlic, ginger paprika, cinnamon and turmeric - the lentils are the real star. They soak up the insanely flavorful spice, provide a toothy texture, and are an earthy counterpoint to the sweet potato and juicy chicken. The buttery, flaky, pastry topper tucks it all in, completing a dish that will decidedly break any meal time rut!

Notes: Green lentils cook up in about 20-25 minutes. If that is not the type of lentil you have, you may need to adjust the cooking time. Check your package instructions.

If you have small, oven safe bowls, you can also make this pot pie into individual portions. Baking time will be slightly less, just keep an eye on the pastry. It is done when puffed and golden brown.

1. Preheat your oven to 400 F.

2. Melt the butter over medium heat in a large pot. Add the onions and a pinch of salt and cook until softened, about 8 minutes. Stir in the garlic, ginger, paprika, cinnamon, turmeric and mint, and cook for 1 minute. Add the lentils, broth and salt and bring to a simmer. Cover and cook for 15 minutes.

3. Stir in the sweet potato and return the lid. Cook for another 12-15 minutes, checking the liquid and adding a little hot water if the sweet potato and lentils are not submerged. When the potato is tender and the lentils cooked through, add the chicken. Taste for seasoning, and add more salt, if needed. *Chicken broths vary widely in their saltiness, even with the low-sodium varieties. Be sure to taste and adjust.* Add plenty of freshly ground black pepper.

4. Pour the mixture into a 9 x 12-inch baking dish. Roll out the puff pastry to fit the baking dish, trimming it if necessary, and pinch it to the sides of the baking dish. Cut three X's in the top with a sharp knife, then place the dish in the preheated oven. Bake for 30 minutes. The pastry should be nicely browned when finished.

5. Remove and let cool for a few minutes, then use a sharp, serrated knife to cut through the pastry, and a large spoon to dish out the filing with the pastry.

SPATCHCOCKED CHICKEN WITH ORANGE TURMERIC ROASTED BRUSSELS & CELERY ROOT

Our first time hosting thanksgiving, we went big! Really big. A 26-pound behemoth from a local farm. It was also the first time we tried spatchcocking - a technique of removing the backbone, flattening the breastbone and splaying the bird for more even cooking. I don't often wear safety goggles in the kitchen, but with that size turkey, let's just say a saw, mallets and perching on counters for leverage were involved... memories to last a lifetime! Ever since then, we've been spatchcocking our turkeys and chickens. Not only do they bake more evenly (so the breasts don't dry out before the legs and thighs are done), but spatchcocking reduces baking time, meaning you can have a perfectly juicy roast chicken in 45 minutes! While the chicken is the star of the show, the vegetable side brings the flavor. Turmeric and orange are heavy hitters, but it's the splash of sherry vinegar that brings the roasted veggies to their full potential.

Serves 6

FOR THE VEGETABLES:

1 ½ pounds celery root, peeled and cut into ½" cubes

1 ½ pounds brussels sprouts, trimmed and halved

4 tablespoons extra virgin olive oil

2 teaspoons kosher salt

3 large garlic cloves, finely chopped

2 teaspoons freshly grated turmeric, or use 1 teaspoon ground

¼ cup fresh orange juice

1 tablespoon sherry vinegar

4 dates, pitted and coarsely chopped

1 teaspoon nigella seeds or black sesame seeds

Freshly cracked black pepper

FOR THE CHICKEN:

1 whole chicken (about 3 ½ pounds)

1 teaspoon kosher salt

1 teaspoon oregano

1 teaspoon garlic powder

1 teaspoon paprika

1 lemon

1. Preheat your oven to 400 F.

2. Place the celery root and brussels sprouts in a large roasting dish, or 10 to12-inch cast iron skillet. Toss with the olive oil and salt. In a separate small bowl, combine the garlic, turmeric, orange juice, vinegar and chopped dates. Do not add the seasoning yet.

3. To prepare the chicken, remove the back bone by cutting along each side of it with kitchen scissors. Discard the back bone, or use for stock. Place the chicken on a baking sheet or in a 12-inch cast iron skillet breast side up. Press down hard on the breast bone, flattening the chicken. Make sure the legs are splayed out to the sides, not tucked under. The goal is to get the chicken as flat as possible.

4. Thinly slice 4 pieces of the lemon, removing any seeds, and tuck two slices between the skin and the breast on each side. Cut the remaining lemon into wedges and place underneath the chicken.

5. Combine the salt, oregano, garlic powder and paprika in a small bowl. Drizzle the chicken with the olive oil, rubbing it in, then rub the spices all over the chicken.

6. Roast the chicken for 15 minutes, then turn the heat down to 375 F and place the vegetables in the oven as well. Stir the vegetables every 10 or 15 minutes. After the vegetables have been roasting for 35-40 minutes, remove them from the oven and test them for doneness. If the celery root is not tender, return them to the oven. When they are cooked thoroughly, remove from the oven and pour in the orange/date mixture while it is hot, stirring to coat.

7. Check the chicken for doneness; a meat thermometer should read 165 F inserted into the thigh, not touching any bone. Once it is cooked through, remove and let rest for 10 minutes before carving. The lemon wedges can be discarded, or served to enjoy alongside the chicken for those who like them. Sprinkle the vegetables with the sesame or nigella seeds and serve them alongside the chicken.

POMEGRANATE GLAZED TURKEY MEATBALLS WITH BAKED BASMATI RICE

This dish has a Middle Eastern vibe, especially with the pomegranate molasses. As with many ethnic ingredients, which once were obscure and difficult to procure, pomegranate molasses is now readily available at large grocery stores. It has a strong, slightly acidic, sweet-tart flavor that adds so much depth with so little effort. A little goes a long way, and you'll love the sweet, sticky coating it lends to this dish. Sometimes I find pomegranate molasses with the other Middle Eastern ingredients; sometimes it's near the baking molasses and maple syrups. Ask for help if you can't find it.

Serves 6

FOR THE MEATBALLS:

1 pound ground turkey

1 cup sourdough bread, crusts removed, cubed or torn into pieces

¼ cup milk

1 egg

1 teaspoon kosher salt

1 teaspoon dried oregano

½ teaspoon ground allspice

½ teaspoon ground cumin

2 tablespoons extra virgin olive oil

FOR THE GLAZE:

¾ cup fresh squeezed orange juice from satsumas or other variety of mandarin orange

3 tablespoons light brown sugar

1 tablespoon pomegranate molasses

3 garlic cloves, grated or chopped finely

FOR THE RICE:

1 ½ cups basmati rice

2 ½ cups boiling water

2 tablespoons unsalted butter, cut into small pieces

1 teaspoon kosher salt

2 small cinnamon sticks

2 large garlic cloves, sliced

½ teaspoon cumin seeds

¼ cup dried cranberries

TO FINISH THE DISH:

½ cup roughly chopped cilantro

¼ cup shelled pistachios, lightly toasted and very coarsely chopped

¾ -1 cup crumbled feta

1. Preheat your oven to 425 F.

2. Begin by making the meatballs. Pour the milk over the bread and let it soak for 5 minutes while you put the rest together. Combine the turkey, egg, oregano, salt, allspice and cumin in a medium bowl. Gently squeeze the excess milk from the bread and add that to the bowl with the turkey (discard any remaining milk). Use your hands to combine it all together, making sure it is thoroughly mixed. Line a plate with parchment paper or rub a little olive oil on the plate, then form the meatballs. *I find having a bowl of water nearby to dip my hands into keeps them from getting too sticky and makes it easier to form the meatballs.* Form them about the size of a golf ball, which should result in 16 meatballs. Set them on the plate. *They can be made a few hours ahead and refrigerated.*

3. Pour the orange juice and sugar in a small skillet or saucepan. Cook at a brisk simmer until reduced by half, then add in the pomegranate molasses and garlic, and cook one more minute. Set aside. *This can also be made ahead and refrigerated.*

4. Combine the rice, cranberries, salt, cinnamon, cumin seed and garlic in a 9 x 9-inch baking dish. Stir to evenly distribute the spices and dot the top with the butter. Pour the boiling water into the dish, then cover very tightly with aluminum foil. It's important to get a good seal otherwise the rice will not cook properly. Place in the preheated oven and bake for 30 minutes.

5. Test the rice for doneness, returning it to the oven if the grains are not fully cooked. Once done, remove to a rack and let sit, covered, for at least 10 minutes.

6. Pour 2 tablespoons of olive oil into a skillet and warm over medium-high heat. Fry the meatballs, turning, until they are cooked through and nicely browned. If they are particularly splattery, cover partially with a lid, which will also help them cook faster. They should take roughly 10 minutes. Pour in the orange pomegranate mixture and cook for 1 more minute stirring to glaze the meatballs.

7. Remove the foil from the rice and discard the cinnamon sticks. Divide between 4 shallow bowls or dinner plates, topping each with 4 meatballs. Drizzle a little bit of sauce over each bowl of rice, then sprinkle with cilantro, pistachios, and 2-3 tablespoons of the feta.

TURKEY ENCHILADAS WITH MAPLE-ROASTED BUTTERNUT SQUASH

Serves 4-6

FOR THE SQUASH:

1 medium butternut squash (about 1 ¼ pounds), peeled, seeded and cut into ½" pieces

2 tablespoons extra virgin olive oil

1 teaspoon ground cinnamon

1 teaspoon ground cumin

1 teaspoon kosher salt

1 tablespoon chopped fresh rosemary

2 tablespoons pure maple syrup

FOR THE TURKEY FILLING:

2 tablespoons extra virgin olive oil

2 medium shallots, chopped

3 large garlic cloves, chopped

1 pound ground turkey

½ teaspoon kosher salt

2 teaspoons ancho chili powder

½ teaspoon cumin seeds or 1 teaspoon ground cumin

1 teaspoon dried oregano

½ teaspoon ground allspice

TO FINISH:

10 flour tortillas, 8-inch size

1 ½ cups shredded mild cheese, such as monterey jack or mozzarella

2 cups tomatillo salsa or green enchilada sauce, mild or medium

¼ cup chopped cilantro

¼ cup chopped white onion

This is the way to do fall enchiladas. Cinnamon-flecked, maple-roasted butternut squash might seem out of place in a savory enchilada, but the garlicky chili and cumin-spiced turkey keep the sweetness in check. Wrapped in soft, flour tortillas, and doused with green salsa for a welcomed acidity, this is one of my favorite ways to enjoy squash in the fall. A hearty, yet healthy dinner.

1. Preheat your oven to 375 F.

2. Place all of the ingredients for the squash except the maple syrup in a large cast iron skillet or baking dish, and toss to combine. Roast for 30-35 minutes until the squash is tender, then add the maple syrup and roast for 5 more minutes. Remove from the oven and reduce the oven temperature to 325 F.

3. While the squash is roasting, cook the turkey. Warm the olive oil in a skillet, and add the shallots and garlic. Cook over medium-low heat for 2-3 minutes until softened. Add the turkey, salt and remaining spices, and cook, breaking up the meat with a spoon. When the meat is fully cooked, combine it with the squash, stirring just to combine.

4. Combine the salsa with the cilantro and onion in a small bowl. Spoon a little of the salsa into a 12 x 9-inch baking dish so that it just covers the bottom. Fill each tortilla evenly with filling, roll up and place in the baking dish seam side down. Cover the enchiladas with the remaining sauce and the cheese.

5. Bake for 15-20 minutes, until the cheese is browned. Serve warm.

CHICKEN TACOS IN CHEATER'S BLACK BEAN MOLE

Mole's are serious business. Almost 20 years ago, I took an intensive chef's course in Oaxaca, Mexico. We spent days learning the intricacies of the regions famous moles, one of which, the mole negro, can take up to two full days to make. Typically, there is a laundry list of ingredients and several steps required to achieve the silky smooth and multi-layered sauce, but in this recipe, I replicate the flavors without the time and fuss. From cinnamon to cumin, cocoa and chili powder, mole has no shortage of zesty ingredients. What makes these tacos pop, though, is the pineapple. It draws out the sweetness from the mole, and its acidity cuts through the richness. Assemble and serve on a platter, or do these tacos DIY-style at the table.

Serves 4

1 small white onion, chopped, divided use

2 large garlic cloves, smashed with the side of a knife

1 tablespoon ancho chili powder

1 tablespoon cocoa powder

1 teaspoon kosher salt

1 teaspoon ground cinnamon

2 ½ teaspoons ground cumin

½ teaspoon ground allspice

⅓ cup red wine vinegar

2 tablespoons olive oil

2 tablespoons pure maple syrup

1 tablespoon tahini

1 cup canned black beans, rinsed and drained

½-¾ cup chicken broth

2 cups cooked chicken, torn into chunky shreds

FOR SERVING THE TACOS:

8-12 corn tortillas, warmed

2 ripe avocados, cut into large cubes

1 cup cilantro, roughly chopped

½ cup jarred or canned pickled jalapeños

1 cup chopped fresh pineapple

Note: I often use a rotisserie chicken for this recipe, or simply grilled or roasted chicken breasts.

1. Begin by organizing your toppings. I like to put them all in one divided serving platter, but if you don't have one that can fit all of the toppings, place the avocado, cilantro, pineapple and jalapeños in separate bowls, each with a small serving spoon. Pop in the fridge until ready to serve.

2. Place ½ cup of the onion, the garlic, chili powder, cocoa powder, salt, cinnamon, 2 teaspoons of the cumin and allspice in a mini food processor. Blend until you have a thick paste, scraping down the sides, if needed. Put the remaining chopped onion in a small bowl or jar. Pour the ⅓ cup of vinegar over the onions, or however much you need to cover them. Set aside on the counter until later.

3. Warm the oil in a medium saucepan. Add the onion/spice mixture and cook over medium-low heat, stirring occasionally, for 2 minutes. Put the black beans in the mini food processor while the paste is cooking (no need to clean it from the mole paste), and blitz them so they are about half broken down. Add them to the pot along with ½ cup of the broth. Stir to scrape up any paste that has stuck to the bottom. Add the maple syrup and tahini and stir to blend well. Cook over low heat, stirring occasionally, for 5 minutes.

4. Add the shredded chicken and remaining ½ teaspoon of cumin, and if it's very thick, add some more broth, but not too much as you do not want the tortillas to be soggy when you fill them. Taste for seasoning, and add more salt, if necessary. Keep warm, covered, over very low heat.

5. Warm the tortillas in a dry skillet, or wrap in foil and warm in an oven. When ready to serve, wrap the tortillas in a kitchen towel and bring to the table with the chicken mole, toppings, and the pickled onions, which you can drain before serving (keeping the vinegar for another use), or serve with a slotted spoon.

A SWEET FINISH: DESSERTS

Sweets, to some, are the best part of the meal. And by some, I mean me…
plus every kid, and just about every kid at heart, I've ever met. I'd say I'm
in good company!

There is always a good reason to indulge in a special treat. From dinner
parties to picnics, holidays to birthdays, and of course, my favorite, "just
because."

My sweets chapter has an option for every occasion. Pizza night? Try the
semifreddo or budino. Taco Tuesday? Piña Colada Popsicles are a must!
Cozy winter holidays call for an incredibly moist and decadent Chocolate
Studded Gingerbread cake. And no birthday is complete without my
showstopper of a cake, cookies 'n cream-style.

Each and every treat brings the zest, *of course*. From a swirl of tahini
in the brownies, to the jammy, roasted strawberries in the cheesecake
mousse. Each will leave you craving *just one more* bite… the ultimate sign
of a successful ending.

Be sure to review my Baking Principles on page **15**, as it contains pointers
for better baking.

LIME SPIKED WHITE CHOCOLATE MACADAMIA COOKIES

Makes 18 cookies

1 ½ cups (192 grams) cake flour

1 ½ cups (192 grams) bread flour

1 teaspoon baking soda

1 teaspoon baking powder

1 teaspoon kosher salt

2 sticks (½ pound) unsalted butter, at room temperature

2 cups (400 grams) granulated sugar

1 egg plus 1 egg yolk, at room temperature

2 teaspoons pure vanilla extract

1 ½ tablespoons lime zest

1 cup white chocolate chips

1 cup macadamia nuts, coarsely chopped

A classic cookie gets zesty... with a boost of fresh lime zest. But the good stuff doesn't stop there - the texture of this cookie is to die for. Overnight refrigeration of the dough is crucial to achieve the right consistency, so plan ahead. It's worth the wait, as they turn out crisp on the outside and just slightly soft on the inside. And with the zest from the lime, sweetness from the white chocolate, and crunch from the nuts, they are oh-so heavenly.

1. In a medium bowl, combine the flours, baking soda, baking powder and salt.

2. Place the sugar and lime zest in the bowl of a stand mixer with the paddle attachment and turn it on low for one minute. Add the softened butter and beat on medium speed until lightened and fluffy, about 5 minutes. Add the egg and egg yolk, then the vanilla, and beat until incorporated. Scrape down the sides and mix again to make sure it is all evenly combined. Add the flour and mix, scraping again, then stir in the chips and nuts.

3. Refrigerate the mixture for at least 2 hours, and preferably overnight.

4. Preheat your oven to 350 F. Use a 1 ½ inch cookie scoop to form the dough into balls and place them 2 inches apart on parchment lined baking sheets. If the dough is too hard to scoop, let it sit at room temperature for 10 or 15 minutes.

5. Bake the cookies for 15 minutes, rotating the pans halfway through, until they are baked through and just starting to get a little color. Remove and place on racks to cool.

Cookies will keep for a week stored at room temperature in an airtight container.

BROWNIE BARS FOR BEACH DAYS

Makes 9 large brownies or 16 small squares

4 ounces bittersweet chocolate

8 tablespoons (1 stick) unsalted butter, plus more for buttering the pan

½ cup (100 grams) light brown sugar

½ cup (100 grams) granulated sugar

2 large eggs at room temperature

1 teaspoon pure vanilla extract

¼ teaspoon kosher salt

⅔ cup (80 grams) all-purpose flour

⅓ cup raspberry preserves, Bon Maman® brand preferred, and seeds strained out if you like

FOR THE TAHINI MIXTURE:

½ cup well stirred tahini

½ cup (100 grams) granulated sugar

1 egg at room temperature

Note: I recommend using Bon Maman brand for the raspberry preserves. It is made with cane sugar instead of high fructose corn syrup, and will have a more tart flavor. Brands that are sweetened with corn syrup proved to be too sweet during testing, and overwhelmed the balance of the flavors. If that is all you can find, cut the amount of preserves to 3 tablespoons. It is important also to use preserves, not jelly.

Growing up in Florida, I spent a lot of time at the beach as a kid, and have the freckles to prove it! Beach fare was always easy... chips, sodas, and peanut butter & jellys. Now, when I daydream of a treat to tote to the beach, or any outdoor gathering, those memories float to the surface. Let's call this the grown-up twist. Swapping tahini for the peanut butter gives these bars added sophistication, and swirling in raspberry jam is, OMG! The most incredible riff on a pb&j. But hey, they're still a brownie, and kids of every age love them. Not as carefree as slathering Jif on some Wonder Bread, but so worth the effort!

1. Preheat your oven to 350 F. Butter an 8 x 8-inch pan and line with parchment paper.

2. Place the chocolate and butter in a heat proof bowl and set it over a pot of barely simmering water (see tip on how to use a double boiler in *Important Techniques*). Stir with a silicone spatula until melted. Remove from the heat and whisk in both sugars. Add the eggs one at a time, then the vanilla and salt. Stir in the flour using the spatula.

3. In a separate bowl, mix together the tahini, sugar and remaining one egg until thoroughly combined. It will be thick.

4. Spread about half of the chocolate batter in the pan, then the tahini mixture evenly over the top of the chocolate batter. It is thick, and using your hands to break it into pieces and distribute the batter is the easiest thing to do. It should mostly cover the brownie batter with a few spaces. Spread the remaining chocolate batter on top, then use a sharp knife to swirl them together. Spoon the jam on top of the batters, dropping teaspoon sized blobs around evenly spaced on top. Use the knife to swirl the raspberry jam just slightly into the batter. The goal is to make sure every square will have a little jam.

5. Bake for 35-40 minutes, until it is no longer jiggly in the middle and the edges look crisp, then remove to a rack to cool. *The brownies are really good when eaten slightly warm (about an hour after baking), but will be delicious for 2-3 days after baking. Store at room temperature, well covered.*

PEPPERMINT CHOCOLATE CHIP RICE KRISPIE SQUARES

Makes 9 large or 16 small squares

8 tablespoons (1 stick) unsalted butter, plus more for buttering the pan

10 ounce bag of mini marshmallows

¼ cup finely ground candy canes (4 standard size), or peppermint candies

¼ teaspoon kosher salt

6 ounces rice cereal (about 6 cups)

½ teaspoon peppermint extract

1 teaspoon pure vanilla extract

½ cup chocolate chips

How does one amp up rice krispie treats... candy canes! Credit for this stroke of genius goes to my son, Miles. One summer afternoon, stashed in the back of our pantry, he discovered leftover candy canes and asked if he could crush them into the batch of rice krispies we were planning to make. We decided to toss in chocolate chips, too, for good measure. Work quickly once you add the chocolate chips - they will begin to melt from the heat of the marshmallow, so it's important to get them in the pan quickly.

1. Butter an 8x8-inch square pan.

2. Melt the butter and marshmallows together in a large saucepan over medium-low heat. Stir with a silicone spatula until fully melted, then add in the ground candies, extracts and salt, and stir. Remove from the heat and stir in the cereal.

3. Working quickly, stir in the chocolate chips and get the mixture in the pan right away. Some of the chips will melt and that's ok. Press down evenly and let cool before cutting into bars.

PIÑA COLADA POPSICLES

Makes 8 popsicles

14 ounce can unsweetened coconut cream (not cream of coconut and not coconut milk)

12 ounces fresh or frozen pineapple

½ cup sugar

½ cup water

⅛ teaspoon salt

Refreshing, light and casual, popsicles are easy going, and easy to make. Here, sweet, tart pineapple is rounded with coconut cream, for a riff on the classic piña colada. Despite the name, these don't call for alcohol - although if the adults would like an additional flavor hit, spike them with a teaspoon or two of rum (note that too much alcohol will inhibit the freezing process). I keep these on hand for my vegan and gluten-free friends, but of course you needn't follow a special diet to enjoy. Coconut cream is generally found near other canned coconut milk products.

1. Bring the water and sugar to a low simmer and stir until the sugar is dissolved. Add the salt and let cool slightly.

2. Pour the coconut cream, sugar water, and pineapple in a large blender. Puree until very smooth, about 3 minutes.

3. Pour into 8 popsicle molds (it may make more or less depending on the size of your popsicle molds). Freeze for at least 6 hours.

KEY LIME PIE NO-CHURN ICE CREAM

Serves 10

FOR THE LIME CURD:

2 large eggs

1 egg yolk

6 tablespoons key lime juice

2 teaspoons key lime zest

½ cup sugar

4 tablespoons (½ stick) unsalted butter, at room temperature

TO MAKE THE ICE CREAM:

14 ounce can sweetened condensed milk

1 teaspoon pure vanilla extract

2 cups whipping cream

3 sheets graham crackers, broken into small pieces

Key limes are prized for being intensely aromatic, slightly floral and very tart. They are often used in very sweet desserts, such as key lime pie (hello sweetened condensed milk!), where their intense tartness and slight bitterness are offset. I love them here in my no-churn ice cream. Do note that key limes are a seasonal fruit, so if you cannot find them, regular limes may be substituted (bump up the amount of zest to a tablespoon).

1. Begin by making the curd. Add the eggs, yolk, juice, zest and sugar to a medium saucepan. Whisk to combine, and place over medium-low heat. Cook, whisking constantly, for 8-10 minutes, turning the heat to low if it looks like it might begin to boil. The mixture can easily overcook on direct heat, so if you are more comfortable, use a double boiler. This method will take longer as the heat is more gentle, but the eggs will not scramble as easily. The mixture is done when it is thick enough that the whisk leaves a trail when dragged through. Remove from the heat and whisk in the butter. Let it cool. *Curd can be made a few days ahead and refrigerated.*

2. Combine the condensed milk and vanilla in a large bowl. In a separate bowl whip the cream until quite thick, but make sure you stop before it turns to butter. You can whip the cream by hand or use beaters. Fold half of the cream into the condensed milk, then fold half of the lime curd into the cream / condensed milk mixture. Finally fold in the remaining whipped cream, and then stir in the broken graham cracker pieces and remaining lime curd, leaving some streaks.

3. Pour into a 9 x 5-inch loaf pan, cover and freeze for at least 6 hours.

MASCARPONE SEMIFREDDO WITH GINGERSNAP BROWN BUTTER CRUMB CRUST

Serves 8-10

FOR THE CRUMB CRUST:

½ cup ground gingersnap cookies (2 ounces), Mi-Del® brand preferred

2 tablespoons unsalted butter

¼ cup raw unsalted pecans, toasted and cooled

FOR THE SEMIFREDDO:

½ cup (4 ounces) mascarpone cheese

1 cup heavy whipping cream

1 ½ tablespoons Marsala, or substitute Madeira

2 tablespoons powdered sugar

3 large egg whites

⅔ cup (133 grams) granulated sugar

¼ teaspoon cream of tartar

1 tablespoon water

A pinch of salt

Similar to ice cream - yet simpler to make - in Italian, semifreddo roughly translates to "half frozen". No churning nor special equipment is required; instead, whipped cream is simply folded in with soft meringue, scooped into a loaf pan and popped in the freezer. Once it sets up, it's slice and serve! My semifreddo includes mascarpone, offering a luxurious mouthfeel and slight tanginess. Marsala, the Sicilian fortified wine, adds a note of sweetness and depth of flavor. For those who would rather not use Marsala, vanilla extract is a fine substitution, however, do note that using fortified wine will result in the best texture, as the alcohol prevents it from freezing too hard. Toasted pecans, brown butter and ground gingersnaps in the crust provide a welcome crunch and textural contrast.

1. Line an 8 x 4-inch loaf pan with plastic wrap, then begin by making the crust. Cook the butter in a small saucepan over medium heat until the butter solids begin to turn brown, stirring with a silicone spatula. It should take a few minutes, and will pop and bubble as it cooks. Remove from the heat when you see the solids begin to turn brown, and pour into a heat proof bowl. *The saucepan will remain hot, and if you left it in there, the butter would continue to cook even off the heat, and could burn.*

2. Grind the cookies in a food processor until they are fine crumbs. Add the pecans and process again until the nuts and cookies are very fine, but stop before the pecans begin to release their oils and become pecan "butter." Add the browned butter, pulse, then press the crumbs into the bottom of the loaf pan.

3. Bring a medium pot of water to a simmer and find a heat proof bowl that fits on top of the pot without touching the water (see tip on how to use a double boiler in *Important Techniques*). Place the egg whites, cream of tartar, granulated sugar, water and pinch of salt in the bowl. Beat, using hand held electric beaters, for 5 minutes over simmering water. The egg whites will become thick and glossy.

Remove from the heat and beat for one more minute to help them start to cool down.

4. Place the mascarpone in a medium bowl and beat with hand held beaters for 1 minute. (You could instead do this in a stand mixer with the whisk attachment). Add the whipping cream and powdered sugar and beat until thickened. Add the Marsala and beat again to combine. The consistency should be like thick whipped cream.

5. If the egg whites are still hot, pop them in the refrigerator for 10-15 minutes to help them cool down. They don't need to be fridge-cold, but if they are warm they will adversely affect the mascarpone cream mixture's texture and consistency. Fold about a cup of the egg whites into the cream to lighten, then add another scoopful and fold that in. Transfer that mixture to the egg whites and continue to gently fold together until it is well combined, being careful to not deflate the egg whites. It should take about 2 minutes.

6. Pour (or scoop) into the prepared loaf pan. Freeze for at least 6 hours. When ready to serve, use the plastic wrap to remove the semifreddo from the pan. Place on a cutting surface and slice into thick pieces and serve immediately.

ORANGE CARAMEL BUDINO

Italian for pudding, a budino is a chilled custard often made with caramel or butterscotch. They're a favorite at Neapolitan pizza joints, and if they're not already on your list, they'll soon be a favorite. The pudding requires a bit of stirring as it comes together, but the upside is a fabulous, do-ahead dinner party finale. What makes this pudding extra special is the orange caramel layer. Think: the ultimate creamsicle!

Serves 6

FOR THE BUDINO:

¼ cup cornstarch

1 egg

2 egg yolks

¼ teaspoon kosher salt

1 ½ cups heavy cream

1 ½ cups whole milk

¾ cup (150 grams) sugar

2 tablespoons corn syrup

2 tablespoons water

5 tablespoons unsalted butter, softened

2 teaspoons pure vanilla extract

1 tablespoon orange liqueur, such as Grand Marnier® or Cointreau®, optional

FOR THE ORANGE CARAMEL:

1 large navel orange

½ cup (100 grams) light brown sugar

¼ cup heavy cream

2 tablespoons unsalted butter, softened

1. Set a fine mesh strainer over a large bowl and set aside.

2. In a medium bowl, whisk the egg, yolks and cornstarch, then whisk in ½ cup of the milk. Set this aside.

3. Make the caramel. Pour the remaining 1 cup milk and 1 ½ cups cream in a pyrex measuring cup or pitcher. Place the sugar, corn syrup and water in a medium saucepan over medium-low heat. Stir very gently with a silicone spatula until the sugar granules are all melted, then increase the heat and bring to a simmer. Cook the sugar mixture, without stirring, until it is a deep amber color. If it is not caramelizing evenly, you can swirl the pan gently. When it is a deep amber color, pour in the milk and cream carefully as it could splatter. It will steam and the sugar will seize. Return the pot to medium heat and stir with a whisk until the sugar melts back into the milk and cream, creating the caramel base.

4. Give the egg/cornstarch/milk mixture a whisk again as the cornstarch will settle. About ¼ cup at a time, pour the caramel base into the bowl with the cornstarch mixture, whisking. This tempers the eggs, bringing them up to a high temperature slowly, so that they don't scramble. Once all the caramel base is incorporated, pour the entire mixture back into the pot. Cook over medium heat, whisking constantly, until it becomes thick like pudding. If you have a thermometer, it should be at least 180 F. The timing for this will likely be between 6-10 minutes, but it could take longer. If you don't have a thermometer, keep a close eye and remove it from the heat as soon as you see one or two bubbles come to the surface.

Immediately remove from the heat and pour through the strainer into the large bowl. Whisk in the vanilla, orange liqueur, if using, and softened butter. Let it cool slightly before pouring into 6 small mason jars or glasses. Cover and refrigerate at least four hours, and up to a day.

5. To make the orange butterscotch sauce, place the brown sugar in a small saucepan. Cut the orange in half and juice half of the orange into the sugar, which should be ⅓ cup. Place over low heat and stir occasionally as it comes up to a simmer. Once the sugar mixture has begun to simmer, let it cook for 7 minutes. Carefully pour in the cream, and cook at a low simmer for another 4 minutes. Remove from the heat and stir in the butter.

6. Use a rasp grater, such as a Microplane, to grate 1 teaspoon of zest from the other half of the orange. Stir this into the orange caramel sauce, then refrigerate the sauce.

7. Place the remaining half orange cut side down on a work surface and use a sharp knife to cut away the peel and pith. Working over a bowl to catch the juices, cut the orange into segments in between the membranes, so that you end up with only the soft juicy middle. Place the segments in the bowl with any juices and refrigerate until ready to serve.

8. When ready to serve, top each budino with equal amounts of the caramel sauce and nestle two or three orange segments into the caramel.

The budino, caramel, and orange segments can be prepared a day ahead, refrigerated separately.

CHEESECAKE MOUSSE WITH ROASTED STRAWBERRY PUREE

Serves 6

12 ounces strawberries, rinsed and hulled, halved or quartered if large

3 tablespoons light brown sugar

2 teaspoons pure vanilla extract

1 teaspoon lemon zest

1 teaspoon lemon juice

¾ teaspoon gelatin

8 ounces (½ pound) cream cheese, at room temperature

⅔ cup plain Greek yogurt

⅔ cup powdered sugar

⅛ teaspoon kosher salt

⅔ cup heavy cream

1 small jar of good quality caramel sauce (you will not use all of it)

2 tablespoons chopped Marcona almonds

All the flavors of cheesecake, but with a no-fuss preparation, and a much more luscious consistency to the thick and creamy mousse. Roasting the strawberries concentrates the juicy, red fruit and adds zest to this dessert. Paired with lemon, the puree lends a sweet, springtime flavor, which perfectly compliments the tangy cream cheese and Greek yogurt in the mousse. Make these ahead, but don't add the caramel or nuts until serving, otherwise the caramel will begin to dissolve and the nuts will lose their crunch.

1. Preheat your oven to 400 F. Toss the strawberries and brown sugar together in a roasting dish and bake for 20 minutes, stirring occasionally. Remove from the oven and allow it to cool slightly while you prepare the cheesecake mousse.

2. Place the cream cheese, yogurt, 1 teaspoon of the vanilla, salt and powdered sugar in a food processor and blend until creamy, scraping down the sides, if necessary.

3. In a separate bowl, beat the heavy cream with electric beaters or by hand until it is a thick whipped cream. Add the cream cheese to the bowl with the whipped cream, and fold together until fully combined. Cover and refrigerate.

4. Place the strawberries and their juices into the food processor (no need to have cleaned it, just give it a good scrape out with the spatula when the cream cheese mixture comes out), and puree with the lemon zest and juice, a pinch of salt and the other one teaspoon of vanilla.

5. Place the gelatin in a small bowl with 1 ½ teaspoons of water and let it soften for 5 minutes. Pour the strawberry puree in a small saucepan and warm over low heat. When it is almost at a simmer, spoon two tablespoons of the warm strawberry puree into the gelatin and whisk so that the gelatin dissolves. Add that back to the strawberries on the stove, whisking to combine, and simmer for 1 minute. Remove and let cool completely.

6. Place 6 jars or glasses on your counter and divide the cheesecake mousse evenly between them. If you like, you could use a piping bag to neatly deposit the mousse into the jars. Next, divide the strawberry puree equally among the jars, which should be about 2 tablespoons per jar. Refrigerate at least one hour and up to 6 hours.

7. To serve, dollop or drizzle 2-3 teaspoons of caramel into each jar and sprinkle with the chopped Marcona almonds.

MANGO MERINGUE PIE

Makes a 9-inch pie

FOR THE CRUST:

11-13 graham cracker sheets (about 7 ounces)

2 tablespoons sugar

½ teaspoon ground allspice

6 tablespoons unsalted butter

FOR THE MANGO CURD:

1 ½ cups (12 ounces) cubed mango, fresh or frozen

½ cup (100 grams) sugar

2 tablespoons fresh lemon juice

1 teaspoon lemon zest

4 egg yolks

4 tablespoons (½ stick) unsalted butter, softened

⅛ teaspoon kosher salt

FOR THE MERINGUE:

4 egg whites

¼ teaspoon cream of tartar

¾ cup (150 grams) sugar

1 teaspoon pure vanilla extract

Sure you've had lemon meringue pie, but wait until you try *mango* meringue pie! A thick mango curd is nestled in a brown butter graham cracker crust - enough of a reason to make this treat right there - but the marshmallowy clouds of meringue make this heavenly. If you are craving this pie outside of mango season, you may substitute frozen mango, or a good quality canned mango pulp. A digital thermometer comes in handy when making the curd, but isn't required.

1. First make the crust. Preheat your oven to 325 F. Melt the butter in a small saucepan over medium heat until the butter solids begin to turn brown, stirring with a silicone spatula. It should take a few minutes, and will pop and bubble as it cooks. Remove from the heat when you see the solids begin to turn brown. If they are getting too dark in the pan, remove the butter to a heat proof bowl so that they don't burn.

2. Grind the graham crackers, sugar and allspice finely in a food processor, then pour in the brown butter, pulsing a few times to combine. Dump the crumbs into a 9-inch pie plate, press evenly on the bottom and up the sides, then bake for 11-12 minutes. Remove and let cool.

3. For the mango curd, puree the mango in a food processor for 2 minutes, stopping to scrape the sides, if needed, until completely smooth. Pour into a metal mixing bowl with the sugar, lemon, zest and egg yolks and set over a pot of simmering water, making sure not to let the bowl touch the water (see tip on how to use a double boiler in *Important Techniques* on page 15). Whisk constantly for 10-12 minutes until thickened. If you have a thermometer it should reach 170 F. Remove from the heat and whisk in the soft butter one tablespoon at a time along with the salt. Pour into the pie crust and let it cool, then refrigerate for at least 2 hours.

4. To make the meringue, place the egg whites and cream of tartar in a stand mixer with the whisk attachment. Beat until stiff peaks (when you lift the beater out of the egg whites, it will form a peak that will hold its shape). Slowly add the sugar, one tablespoon at a time, then let it beat at medium-high speed for another two minutes, which will help dissolve the sugar. When it is all incorporated, add the vanilla.

5. Spoon the meringue gently on top of the mango curd. Spread it out carefully over the curd (using an offset spatula is the easiest way to do this), making sure it touches the graham cracker crust all around the edges. You can do some decorative swirls on top if you like. Place it in a 350 F oven and bake for 10-12 minutes until lightly browned, then remove to a rack. The pie can be served right away or refrigerated for another few hours.

WHISKEY SOAKED PEACH SKILLET CAKE

I first developed this as an upside down cake, when my then 5 year old son had an infatuation with all cakes upside down. Our family enjoyed it this way for years before we decided to turn it on its (figurative and literal) head! We all craved more texture - a crunchy, crumbly top to complement the juicy, sweet peaches. Right side up was an easy fix! The combination of peaches, pecans and whiskey is an ode to southern flavors, in the most delicious way.

Serves 8-10

FOR THE CRUMBLE TOPPING:

½ cup finely ground pecans

½ cup (100 grams) light brown sugar

2 tablespoons (15 grams) all-purpose flour

½ teaspoon ground ginger

¼ teaspoon ground nutmeg

⅛ teaspoon kosher salt

2 tablespoons unsalted butter, melted

Note: I recommend a 9-inch cast iron skillet for this, but a well buttered 9-inch springform pan will also work, though it will not give you the same crispy edges of the cast iron.

FOR THE CAKE:

1 pound ripe peaches (about 4 large), peeled and cut into wedges

¼ cup whiskey

8 tablespoons (1 stick) unsalted butter, softened, divided use

¾ cup plus 2 tablespoons (175 grams) granulated sugar

2 large eggs at room temperature

1 teaspoon pure vanilla extract

1 ½ cups (180 grams) all-purpose flour

1 teaspoon baking powder

¼ teaspoon baking soda

½ teaspoon kosher salt

½ cup buttermilk

FOR SERVING:

Caramel or vanilla ice cream

1. Preheat your oven to 350 F.

2. Slice the peaches thinly and place them in a bowl with the whiskey. Toss to coat and set them aside to soak.

3. Next prepare the crumble topping. Combine the pecans, brown sugar, flour, ginger, nutmeg and salt in a bowl. Melt two tablespoons of butter in the cast iron skillet, if using. Otherwise melt the butter in a small pan or microwave. Pour the melted butter into the pecan mixture and stir well to combine.

4. Put two more tablespoons of butter in the skillet and melt, brushing it up the sides. If using a springform pan, skip this step and use softened butter to grease the bottom and sides.

5. Now make the cake batter. In a small bowl, whisk together the flour, baking powder, baking soda and salt and set aside.

6. Using a hand-held or stand mixer, beat the remaining 6 tablespoons of softened butter and white sugar together. Add eggs one at a time, scraping the sides and mixing until well combined. Add half of the flour mixture, then all of the buttermilk and the vanilla, then the remaining flour, mixing after each addition. Beat until just combined.

7. Pour the batter into the skillet or prepared pan and spread evenly. It's easiest to do this with an offset spatula. Top with the peaches, making sure to lay them evenly over the batter, and pour any extra liquid from the bowl over the peaches. Scatter with the pecan mixture in an even layer and place in your preheated oven.

8. Bake for 30-35 minutes, until the top of the cake is springy to the touch. Let it cool for 5 minutes in the pan, then serve warm with ice cream.

The cake can be made up to three hours ahead and kept at room temperature. Gently rewarm in a low oven before serving.

"BANANAS FOSTER" STICKY TOFFEE PUDDING

A classic British dessert, sticky toffee pudding is a deeply comforting, warm and gooey dessert to dig into on a chilly evening. (To clear any confusion, across the pond, Brits refer to their dessert as *pudding*, and what we call pudding, as *custard.*) My recipe is a date-sweetened, dark and rich banana cake that is bathed in a rum butterscotch sauce, and topped with a scoop of cool vanilla ice cream and chopped walnuts. The ultimate play on another classic, Bananas Foster.

Serves 9

FOR THE CAKE:

4 tablespoons (½ stick) unsalted butter, at room temperature, plus more for buttering the pan

¾ cup boiling water

1 cup pitted dates (6 ounces), chopped

1 teaspoon baking soda

1 ½ cup (180 grams) all purpose flour

1 teaspoon baking powder

1 teaspoon ground cinnamon

½ teaspoon ground nutmeg, preferably freshly grated

½ teaspoon kosher salt

¾ cup (150 grams) granulated sugar

2 large eggs at room temperature

⅔ cup bananas (about 2 medium), very ripe

1 teaspoon pure vanilla extract

FOR THE SAUCE:

½ cup heavy cream

½ cup (110 grams) dark brown sugar

4 tablespoons (½ stick) unsalted butter

1 tablespoon dark rum

FOR SERVING:

Vanilla ice cream and toasted chopped walnuts (½ cup)

1. Preheat your oven to 350 F. Butter an 8-inch square cake pan with at least 2-inch high sides and set aside.

2. Pour the boiling water over the chopped dates and stir in the baking soda.

3. Combine the flour, baking powder, cinnamon, nutmeg and salt in a medium bowl, and whisk to ensure even distribution.

4. Cream the butter and sugar in a stand mixer using the paddle attachment for about 2 minutes. Add the eggs one at a time and scrape down the sides of the bowl after incorporating, then beat for another 2 minutes and add the vanilla. Add roughly a third of the flour mixture and mix, then half of the bananas and the date mixture and beat again at medium-low speed just until combined. Add another third of the flour, then the remaining bananas and dates, and finally the remaining flour, mixing after each addition. Scrape the sides and bottom, then mix briefly one final time. Don't overmix the batter, but make sure it is all well combined.

5. Pour into the prepared pan and bake for 25-30 minutes until it just starts to pull away from the sides and is springy to the touch.

6. While the cake is baking, make the sauce. In a small saucepan, warm the cream and the brown sugar over medium-low heat. Stir until the sugar is dissolved, about 4 minutes, then whisk in the softened butter, stirring until it is incorporated. Remove from the heat and stir in the rum.

7. When the cake is done, let it cool on a rack. Once cool, using a skewer or small knife, poke holes around the cake, being careful not to tear it. Pour half of the sauce over the cake and let it sit for at least 15 minutes.

8. To serve, gently rewarm the cake in a low oven for a few minutes. I like to do 250 F for around 10 minutes. Cut into 9 pieces, plate, and top with more sauce, ice cream and walnuts.

Leftover cake keeps well at room temperature for a day, or in the refrigerator for 3-4 days.

CRANBERRY FRIAND

Serves 6

FOR THE CRANBERRIES:

8 ounces fresh or frozen cranberries

1 cup (200 grams) granulated sugar

1 cinnamon stick

½ vanilla bean, or substitute 1 teaspoon pure vanilla extract

FOR THE CAKE:

⅓ cup (53 grams) all-purpose flour

1 ⅔ cup (200 grams) powdered sugar

1 cup (120 grams) almond flour

⅛ teaspoon salt

5 large egg whites

12 tablespoons (1 ½ sticks) unsalted butter, melted, plus more for buttering the dish

Vanilla or caramel ice cream for serving

Popular in Australia and New Zealand, friands are absolutely beloved in our household. They are at once sophisticated and nuanced, yet cozy and comforting. As these almondy cakes are also relatively quick to put together, they fall into my "emergency dessert" category. (Official definition: *I NEED dessert tonight, one that I know will bring me utter joy, and that can be made last minute with ingredients I have on hand.*) I call for cranberries in this recipe, though friands can be made with most fruit. What makes this friand next level is the whole vanilla bean. A splurge ingredient for sure, those little dark flecks - the telltale sign of whole bean - together with the tart cranberries and incredibly moist cake, are divine. Serve with a scoop of ice cream, which mellows the cranberries and adds a creamy counterpoint. Pure vanilla extract can be substituted, though it will not impart the same flavor.

1. Place cranberries, granulated sugar and the cinnamon stick in a medium saucepan with 1 tablespoon of water. Split the vanilla bean in half lengthwise, scrape the seeds from each side of the vanilla bean and add to the pot, then throw in the split pod as well. Cook over medium heat for 10-15 minutes, until half the cranberries are broken down and it is thick and syrupy. Remove from the heat and let cool slightly while you prepare the rest of the cake.

2. Preheat the oven to 400 F. Butter a 12-inch square baking dish or a 9 x 13-inch dish.

3. In a small bowl, whisk together the flour, almond flour, powdered sugar, and salt.

4. In a separate bowl, whisk the egg whites until frothy, about 1-2 minutes. Stir in the flour mixture and the melted butter mixing until just combined.

5. Pour the mixture into the prepared baking dish. Remove the cinnamon stick and vanilla pod from the cranberries, then spoon them over top of the batter and place in the preheated oven. Begin checking after 35 minutes. If it starts to darken too much before the center is set, tent the baking dish with foil and continue to bake. It could take up to 45 minutes.

6. Let the cake sit 10 minutes before serving, or up to 40 minutes. Serve warm with ice cream.

CHOCOLATE STUDDED GINGERBREAD BUNDT WITH BOURBON GLAZE

Rich, dark molasses, two kinds of ginger, and warming spices are a good start. But what makes this bundt stellar... chocolate! The heady ingredients are at once tamed and complemented by the luscious, dark chocolate. It's important to scatter the chips on top of the batter before baking, rather than mixing them in. This allows the chocolate to slowly sink into the cake as it bakes; otherwise, they will sink to the bottom and stick to the pan, making the cake difficult to remove.

Serves 10

FOR THE CAKE:

1 cup water

1 cup molasses, not blackstrap

½ teaspoon baking soda

2 cups (240 grams) all-purpose flour

¼ cup (25 grams) unsweetened cocoa powder

1 teaspoon baking powder

½ teaspoon kosher salt

1 teaspoon ground ginger

1 teaspoon ground cinnamon

¼ teaspoon ground cloves

¼ teaspoon ground nutmeg

1 cup (200 grams) light brown sugar, packed

¼ cup (50 grams) granulated sugar

12 tablespoons (1 ½ sticks) unsalted butter, melted and cooled, plus extra for buttering the pan

3 large eggs at room temperature

1 teaspoon freshly grated ginger

½ cup mini bittersweet chocolate chips

Cocoa powder for dusting the baking pan

FOR THE GLAZE:

1 cup (130 grams) powdered sugar

1 teaspoon bourbon or whiskey, or substitute vanilla extract

1-2 tablespoons whole milk

Optional mini chocolate chips for garnish

1. Preheat your oven to 350 F. Generously butter a standard 10-cup bundt pan and dust with cocoa powder, knocking out the excess.

2. Warm the water and molasses in a medium saucepan until it just begins to simmer. Turn off the heat, then whisk in the baking soda. *Be careful as it could bubble up and over. Using a larger pot than you think you need is a good idea to prevent spills.*

3. Whisk together the flour, cocoa powder, baking powder, salt and spices in a medium bowl.

4. Combine both sugars and melted butter in a large bowl and whisk well. Add the fresh grated ginger, then whisk in the eggs. Add half of the flour mixture and whisk to combine, then all the molasses mixture and whisk again, and finally the remaining flour, and combine well.

5. Pour into the prepared pan. Sprinkle the chocolate chips evenly over the top of the batter. They will sink as it bakes. *If you add them to the batter, they* *sink to the bottom and stick to the pan, causing the cake to stick and making it very difficult to remove. By sprinkling them on top, they slowly distribute throughout the cake as it bakes.*

6. Bake for 45 minutes. Using a wooden skewer as a tester, it should have some moist crumbs clinging to it when inserted into the cake, and the cake should slightly pull away from the sides. It will feel springy if you carefully touch the top. Cool in the pan on a rack for 10 minutes, then invert onto the cooling rack to let it cool completely.

7. Combine the powdered sugar, bourbon and milk in a small bowl and whisk. Once the cake has cooled, pour it over top, letting it drip down the sides. If you like, you can serve the cake with a little whipped cream or ice cream.

Well wrapped, cake will keep at room temperature for 3 days.

COOKIES 'N CREAM BIRTHDAY CAKE

Take a classic cream cheese frosting, mix in a bunch of crushed up Oreos, and enter cookies 'n cream heaven. Now, slather that on a perfectly moist, buttermilk chocolate cake, with a handful of cookies mixed into the batter for good measure, and we're talkin' zesty! If you want to go even further, use mint flavored chocolate sandwich cookies. You'll be doing back flips! Be warned, this yields a large cake that will certainly feed a crowd. Leftovers freeze beautifully, or halve the recipe if you prefer.

Serves 12

2 cups (240 grams) all-purpose flour

¾ cup (75 grams) unsweetened cocoa powder, plus more for dusting

1 ½ teaspoons baking powder

½ teaspoon baking soda

½ teaspoon kosher salt

2 sticks (½ pound) unsalted butter, at room temperature

1 ½ cups (300 grams) granulated sugar

4 large eggs at room temperature

1 cup buttermilk

8 chocolate cream-filled sandwich cookies, such as Oreo® or Newman-O's®, crushed finely in a food processor or by hand

FOR THE FROSTING:

1 pound cream cheese, at room temperature

8 tablespoons (1 stick) unsalted butter, at room temperature

⅛ teaspoon salt

3 ½ cups (455 grams) powdered sugar, sifted if lumpy

2 teaspoons pure vanilla extract

12-16 chocolate cream-filled sandwich cookies (should measure about 1 ½ cups)

1. Preheat the oven to 350 F. Butter two 9-inch round cake pans, and line the bottoms with parchment paper. Butter the parchment and dust the cake pan with a little cocoa powder, tapping out the excess. Set aside.

2. In a medium bowl, whisk together the flour, cocoa powder, baking powder, baking soda and salt.

3. In a stand mixer using the paddle attachment, cream the butter and sugar until light and fluffy, about 2-3 minutes. Add the eggs one at a time, scraping the sides of the bowl to make sure they are evenly incorporated.

4. Add a third of the flour mixture, then half of the buttermilk. Scrape the sides and mix again, then add another third of the flour mixture, followed by the remaining buttermilk, then the remaining flour, mixing after each addition. Scrape the bowl again, and finally add the crushed cookie crumbs. Mix with a spatula.

5. Divide the batter equally between the two pans and smooth the top. Bake for 25 minutes, or until the top feels springy and the cake has slightly pulled away from the sides. Cool in the pan on a rack for 10 minutes, then turn out onto the racks to cool completely, removing the parchment paper.

6. To make the frosting: In a stand mixer or using handheld electric beaters, beat the cream cheese, butter and salt together until mixed thoroughly. Add the powdered sugar ½ cup at a time, scraping the bowl as necessary. Add the vanilla and mix, then stir in the cookies until just combined.

7. Once cool, place one layer on your cake plate flat side down. If the cake is very domed, you can trim it with a serrated knife so that it is flat along the top. Spread the frosting on this layer so that it is about ¼ inch thick, then place the second layer on top, trimming again, if needed. Frost the top and sides with the remaining frosting.

Cake can be refrigerated for a day, and brought back to room temperature before serving. Store leftovers in the refrigerator, or freeze for up to a month.

ACKNOWLEDGMENTS

This book would not be possible without my husband, Justin. He challenges me, supports me, pushes me and loves me through triumph and failure. He's the *business* of our duo, freeing me to be the *creative*; the man behind the curtain making the machine hum so that I can be in the kitchen doing my magic. It almost feels strange to thank him in the acknowledgments, as I feel this book is as much his as mine.

A big shout out to my kids, Lucy, Dylan and Miles, for being my biggest cheerleaders, and for always being willing to eat whatever I put in front of them.

To my mom and dad, Aldona & Robert Beall, for instilling in me a love of food and cooking, and exposing me to the glories of different cuisines of the world at an early age.

To the ladies of my Cookbook Club- my sassy, food-loving gals who are an incredible support network, and some of my best recipe testers.

Speaking of testers, you all rock! The book would not be what it is without you. To my star testers, who each made dozens of recipes, helping me perfect each and every one, I express my deepest gratitude. You approached this project with love, dedication and honesty - and your efforts are appreciated more than you know:

Deena Kirsh Taylor, Jennifer Mani, Aldona K. Beall, Michelle Bittle, Smit family, Leslie Wellauer, Elizabeth Dosher, Sara Kupchella, Mary-Peirce Griffith, Ashley Webster, Lydia Moriarty, Zaniello family, Matt Gibbs, Kristin Neilson, Jen Gale, Jo & Grant Angwin, Lauren Hanley.

And to my broader team of recipe testers, who graciously took part, providing tasting notes, catching typos and helping me to fine tune my recipe instructions, I thank you dearly:

Katherine Gudgel, Phyllis Janofsky, Kathleen Kregel, Lindsay Marsh, Ann Martin, Shira Gura, Jean Steinman, Aaron Baum, Scott Roth, Cheryl Nephew, Lynn Pohl, Ken and Sharon Roth, Whitney Zoller Hyde, James Kirsh, Kate Lemery, Elsjebe Mostert, Caroline Rosen, Kristina Amerikaner, Tricia Piho, S. A. (Sam) McNally, Kathy Lusk-Blanche, Leang family, Michaela McCoy, Lily McCoy, Leslie Denker, Pam Hill, Jill Joost Skidmore, Carol Ayers, Garrard/Hartley family, Susan Las, MarshaKay Kirkland , Kristi Marsh, Hitchins family, Joan & Peter Colbert, Lewis family, Anna Pillman, Marcia Turpyn, Shelly Botkin, Michelle Hoyles, Mette Axboe, Grier Ferguson, Cady Ferguson, Maggi Ridolfo, Melanie Smith, Braatz family, Ginger Blane, Laurie Taylor, Krystel Beall, Haley Lebsack, Laura Matos, Fran Borden, Jen LeMaster, Patricia Kelly, Janell Kurchinski, Jonathan Bates, Jan Kirsh, Waller family, Patrick & Meg Keller, Roselle Thomas, Tricia Bromley, Kammie Ward, Berry family, Ginny Detterbeck, Lynne Shapiro, Gail Norry, Roberta Israelsky, Jessica Guten, Courtney Cohen + Mom & Milo Laurich, Kathie Rosso, Kathy Levinson, Julie Wrathall-Alvarez, Bowser family, Michele Reiss-Taylor, Abby Cometz, Christy Dockery Bailey, Shannon Boxley.

INDEX

Carrots:
Salmon Bánh Mi 67
White Bean & Celery Root Soup with Sausage 58
Cauliflower:
Cauliflower Carbonara 101
Honey Ricotta Naan with Roasted Cauliflower 84
Celery Root:
Spatchcocked Chicken with Orange Turmeric Roasted Brussels & Celery Root 134
White Bean & Celery Root Soup with Sausage 58
Cheese:
See blue cheese; cream cheese; feta; fontina; goat cheese; gorgonzola; gruyere; manchego; monterey jack; mozzarella; parmigiano; stilton
Cheesecake Mousse with Roasted Strawberry Puree 158
Cherry Ginger Vodka Cooler 87
Chicken:
Almost a Döner Wrap - Mediterranean Style 64
Chicken Tacos in Cheater's Black Bean Mole 140
Farro Salad with Chicken, Mandarin Oranges, Avocado, Feta & Pistachios 53
Moroccan Spiced Chicken Pot Pie 133
Spatchcocked Chicken with Orange Turmeric Roasted Brussels & Celery Root 134
Chicken Broth:
Brothy Tofu & Rice Noodle Soup 54
Chicken Tacos in Cheater's Black Bean Mole 140
Creamy Baked Orecchiette with Jerusalem Artichokes 112
Indian Butter Tofu with Squash & Chickpeas 129
Moroccan Spiced Chicken Pot Pie 133
Seared Scallops with Basil Mint Pesto & Lemony Artichoke Risotto 118
White Bean & Celery Root Soup with Sausage 58
Chickpeas:
Almost a Döner Wrap - Mediterranean Style 64
Indian Butter Tofu with Squash & Chickpeas 129
Eggplant "Meatballs" with Spaghetti 104
Chili Oil:
Whipped Feta Dip with Mint Chili Oil 72
Chilis:
See chipotle; guajillo; jalapeño; serrano
Chipotle Chilis:
Breakfast Tacos with a Kick 38
Grilled Shrimp Basted in Peach Bourbon BBQ Sauce 126
Chocolate:
Brownie Bars for Beach Days 147
Chocolate-Chocolate Breakfast Bread 22
Chocolate Studded Gingerbread Bundt with Bourbon Glaze 168

Cookies 'n Cream Birthday Cake 170
Peppermint Chocolate Chip Rice Krispie Squares 149
Chocolate Cream-Filled Sandwich Cookies:
Cookies 'n Cream Birthday Cake 170
Cilantro:
Breakfast Tacos with a Kick 38
Brothy Tofu & Rice Noodle Soup 54
Chicken Tacos in Cheater's Black Bean Mole 140
Creamy Tomatillo Avocado Dip 80
Crispy Coconut Fish with Sesame Broccoli & Udon Noodles 116
Herby Zucchini Phyllo Pie 98
Indian Butter Tofu with Squash & Chickpeas 129
Pomegranate Glazed Turkey Meatballs with Baked Basmati Rice 136
Turkey Enchiladas with Maple-Roasted Butternut Squash 139
Salmon Bánh Mi 67
Cocktails:
See Drinks
Cocoa Powder:
Chicken Tacos in Cheater's Black Bean Mole 140
Chocolate-Chocolate Breakfast Bread 22
Chocolate Studded Gingerbread Bundt with Bourbon Glaze 168
Cookies 'n Cream Birthday Cake 170
Hot Eggplant Sandwich with Goat Cheese & a Fried Egg 62
Coconut, toasted:
Crispy Coconut Fish with Sesame Broccoli & Udon Noodles 116
Mango Macadamia Muesli 31
Coconut Cream:
Piña Colada Popsicles 150
Coconut Milk:
Indian Butter Tofu with Squash & Chickpeas 129
Coconut Oil:
Maple Cashew Granola 25
Coconut Sugar:
Brothy Tofu & Rice Noodle Soup 54
Cod Stewed with Roasted Tomatoes, Chilis & Olives 123
Salmon Bánh Mi 67
Sweet & Spicy Asian Shrimp 86
Cod Stewed with Roasted Tomatoes, Chilis & Olives 123
Cookies 'n Cream Birthday Cake 170
Compound Butter:
Foolproof Cacio e Pepe 110
Corn:
Romaine with Corn, Blackberries, Manchego & Pumpkin Seeds 47
Cranberries:
Cranberry Friand 166
Pomegranate Glazed Turkey Meatballs with Baked Basmati Rice 136

Cream:
Bay Scallop "Chowder" Pizza 94
"Bananas Foster" Sticky Toffee Pudding 164
Cheesecake Mousse with Roasted Strawberry Puree 158
Key LIme Pie No-Churn Ice Cream 152
Mascarpone Semifreddo with Gingersnap Brown Butter Crumb Crust 154
Orange Caramel Budino 156
Overnight French Toast with Pear Maple Syrup 32
Whipped Tarragon Goat Cheese 68
Cream Cheese:
Cookies 'n Cream Birthday Cake 170
Cheesecake Mousse with Roasted Strawberry Puree 158
Creme de Cassis:
Summertime Aperitivo 78
Cucumber:
Lexi's G&T 85
Salmon Bánh Mi 67
Tzatziki 64
Crystallized Ginger:
Gingerbread Granola 27

D

Dates:
"Bananas Foster" Sticky Toffee Pudding 164
Spatchcocked Chicken with Orange Turmeric Roasted Brussels & Celery Root 134
Desserts:
"Bananas Foster" Sticky Toffee Pudding 164
Brownie Bars for Beach Days 147
Cheesecake Mousse with Roasted Strawberry Puree 158
Chocolate Studded Gingerbread Bundt with Bourbon Glaze 168
Cranberry Friand 166
Cookies 'n Cream Birthday Cake 170
Key LIme Pie No-Churn Ice Cream 152
Lime Spiked White Chocolate Macadamia Cookies 144
Mango Meringue Pie 160
Mascarpone Semifreddo with Gingersnap Brown Butter Crumb Crust 154
Orange Caramel Budino 156
Peppermint Chocolate Chip Rice Krispie Squares 149
Piña Colada Popsicles 150
Whiskey Soaked Peach Skillet Cake 162
Dill:
Almost a Döner Wrap - Mediterranean Style 64
Herby Zucchini Phyllo Pie 98
Dressings:
Fig Jam Vinaigrette 48
Lime Vinaigrette 50
Orange Balsamic Vinaigrette 42
Shallot vinaigrette 47
Domaine de Canton:
Cherry Ginger Vodka Cooler 87

P

Pancetta:
Garlicky Kale Panini with Sweet Tomato Jam, Gruyere & Pancetta 61
Parmigiano:
Bay Scallop "Chowder" Pizza 94
Braised Fennel & Pine Nut Linguine 102
Cauliflower Carbonara 101
Cod Stewed with Roasted Tomatoes, Chilis & Olives 123
Creamy Baked Orecchiette & Jerusalem Artichokes 112
Eggplant "Meatballs" with Spaghetti 104
Fettuccine with Seared Calamari & Pan Roasted Tomatoes 108
Fool-Proof Cacio e Pepe 110
Haricots Verts in Fig Jam Vinaigrette with Shaved Parmigiano, Hazelnuts & Crispy Prosciutto 48
Porcini Pesto Polenta with Sausage & Leeks 131
Seared Scallops with Basil Mint Pesto & Lemony Artichoke Risotto 118
Parsley:
Eggplant "Meatballs" with Spaghetti 104
Porcini Pesto Polenta with Sausage & Leeks 131
Pasta:
Braised Fennel & Pine Nut Linguine 102
Cauliflower Carbonara 101
Creamy Baked Orecchiette & Jerusalem Artichokes 112
Crispy Coconut Fish with Sesame Broccoli & Udon Noodles 116
Eggplant "Meatballs" with Spaghetti 104
Fettuccine with Seared Calamari & Pan Roasted Tomatoes 108
Foolproof Cacio e Pepe 110
Sweet Potato Pierogi 106
Peas:
Cauliflower Carbonara 101
Peaches:
Beet, Avocado & Kale Salad with Pickled Peaches & Orange Balsamic Vinaigrette 42
Grilled Shrimp Basted with Peach Bourbon BBQ Sauce 126
Whiskey Soaked Peach Skillet Cake 162
Pears:
Overnight French Toast with Pear Maple Syrup 32
Prosciutto Wrapped Roasted Pears 82
Pecans:
Gingerbread Granola 27
Mascarpone Semifreddo with Gingersnap Brown Butter Crumb Crust 154
Rosemary Roasted Mixed Nuts 76
Spiced Apple Butter Oatmeal with Pecans 28
Whiskey Soaked Peach Skillet Cake 162
Peppermint Chocolate Chip Rice Krispie Squares 149
Phyllo:
Herby Zucchini Phyllo Pie 98
Piña Colada Popsicles 150

Pineapple:
Chicken Tacos in Cheater's Black Bean Mole 140
Piña Colada Popsicles 150
Pine Nuts:
Herby Zucchini Phyllo Pie 98
Braised Fennel & Pine Nut Linguine 102
Porcini Pesto Polenta with Sausage & Leeks 131
Pistachios:
Pomegranate Glazed Turkey Meatballs with Baked Basmati Rice 136
Pizza:
Bay Scallop "Chowder" Pizza 94
Bee Sting Pizza 96
Plums:
Summertime Plum, Tomato & Blue Cheese Caprese 44
Polenta:
Porcini Pesto Polenta with Sausage & Leeks 131
Pomegranate Glazed Turkey Meatballs with Baked Basmati Rice 136
Porcini Pesto Polenta with Sausage & Leeks 131
Prosciutto:
Cheesy Baked Asparagus Frittata Topped with Prosciutto 37
Haricots Verts in Fig Jam Vinaigrette with Shaved Parmigiano, Hazelnuts & Crispy Prosciutto 48
Prosciutto Wrapped Roasted Pears 82
Pumpkin Seeds:
Romaine with Corn, Blackberries, Manchego & Pumpkin Seeds 47
Puff Pastry:
Caramelized Endive Tart Tatin 92
Moroccan Spiced Chicken Pot Pie 133

R

Raisins:
Honey Ricotta Naan with Roasted Cauliflower 84
Raspberries:
Lemon Raspberry Muffins 20
Rice:
Indian Butter Tofu with Squash & Chickpeas 129
Pomegranate Glazed Turkey Meatballs with Baked Basmati Rice 136
Seared Scallops with Basil Mint Pesto & Lemony Artichoke Risotto 118
Rice Noodles:
Brothy Tofu & Rice Noodle Soup 54
Ricotta:
Honey Ricotta Naan with Roasted Cauliflower 84
Romaine with Corn, Blackberries, Manchego & Pumpkin Seeds 47
Rosemary:
Braised Fennel & Pine Nut Linguine 102
Cauliflower Carbonara 101
Porcini Pesto Polenta with Sausage & Leeks 131

Roasted Cherry Tomato & Butternut Squash Salad with Lime Vinaigrette 50
Rosemary Roasted Mixed Nuts 76
Shallot vinaigrette 47
Simple Focaccia Bread 125
Sweet Potato Pierogi 106
Tuna Pâté with Sundried Tomatoes 74
Turkey Enchiladas with Maple-Roasted Butternut Squash 139
Rum:
"Bananas Foster" Sticky Toffee Pudding 164
Gingery Hot Spiked Apple Cider 77

S

Saba:
Summertime Plum, Tomato & Blue Cheese Caprese 44
Sage:
Mushroom Leek Soup with Cashew Cream 56
Salads:
Beet, Avocado & Kale Salad with Pickled Peaches & Orange Balsamic Vinaigrette 42
Haricots Verts in Fig Jam Vinaigrette with Shaved Parmigiano, Hazelnuts & Crispy Prosciutto 48
Farro Salad with Chicken, Mandarin Oranges, Avocado, Feta & Pistachios 53
Roasted Cherry Tomato & Butternut Squash Salad with Lime Vinaigrette 50
Romaine with Corn, Blackberries, Manchego & Pumpkin Seeds 47
Summertime Plum, Tomato & Blue Cheese Caprese 44
Salmon:
Orange Miso Roasted Salmon & Blistered Sesame Green Beans 120
Salmon Bánh Mi 67
Sandwiches:
Almost a Döner Wrap - Mediterranean Style 64
Garlicky Kale Panini with Sweet Tomato Jam, Gruyere & Pancetta 61
Hot Eggplant Sandwich with Goat Cheese & a Fried Egg 62
Salmon Bánh Mi 67
Smoked Trout, Heirloom Tomato & Whipped Tarragon Goat Cheese Tartine 68
Sausage:
Porcini Pesto Polenta with Sausage & Leeks 131
White Bean & Celery Root Soup with Sausage 58
Savory Grain Bowl with Crispy Egg & Avocado 34
Scallions:
Smoked Trout, Heirloom Tomato & Whipped Tarragon Goat Cheese Tartine 68
Scallops:
Bay Scallop "Chowder" Pizza 94
Seared Scallops with Basil Mint Pesto & Lemony Artichoke Risotto 118

Serrano Chili:
Brothy Tofu & Rice Noodle Soup 54
Indian Butter Tofu with Squash & Chickpeas 129
Sherry Vinegar:
Farro Salad with Chicken, Mandarin Oranges, Avocado, Feta & Pistachios 53
Spatchcocked Chicken with Orange Turmeric Roasted Brussels & Celery Root 134
Shrimp:
Grilled Shrimp Basted with Peach Bourbon BBQ Sauce 126
Sweet & Spicy Asian Shrimp 86
Smoked Paprika:
Shallot vinaigrette 47
Garlicky Kale Panini with Sweet Tomato Jam, Gruyere & Pancetta 61
Smoked Trout, Heirloom Tomato & Whipped Tarragon Goat Cheese Tartine 68
Soups:
Brothy Tofu & Rice Noodle Soup 54
Mushroom Leek Soup with Cashew Cream 56
White Bean & Celery Root Soup with Sausage 58
Sour Cream:
Harissa Lamb Quesadillas with Lime Crema 88
Sweet Potato Pierogi 106
Spinach:
Roasted Cherry Tomato & Butternut Squash Salad with Lime Vinaigrette 50
Sriracha:
Salmon Bánh Mi 67
Stilton:
Summertime Plum, Tomato & Blue Cheese Caprese 44
Strawberries:
Cheesecake Mousse with Roasted Strawberry Puree 158
Sunchokes:
See Jerusalem Artichokes
Sundried Tomatoes:
Tuna Pâté with Sundried Tomatoes 74
Sunflower Seeds:
Crispy Coconut Fish with Sesame Broccoli & Udon Noodles 116
Sweet Potatoes:
Brothy Tofu & Rice Noodle Soup 54
Moroccan Spiced Chicken Pot Pie 133
Sweet Potato Pierogi 106

T

Tacos:
Breakfast Tacos with a Kick 38
Chicken Tacos in Cheater's Black Bean Mole 140
Tahini:
About 18
Brownie Bars for Beach Days 147
Chicken Tacos in Cheater's Black Bean Mole 140

Tarragon:
Smoked Trout, Heirloom Tomato & Whipped Tarragon Goat Cheese Tartine 68
Tequila:
Mexican 75 89
One Tequila, Two Tequila 81
Thyme:
Bay Scallop "Chowder" Pizza 94
Cheesy Baked Asparagus Frittata Topped with Prosciutto 37
Creamy Baked Orecchiette & Jerusalem Artichokes 112
White Bean & Celery Root Soup with Sausage 58
Tofu:
Brothy Tofu & Rice Noodle Soup 54
Tomatillos:
Creamy Tomatillo Avocado Dip 80
Turkey Enchiladas with Maple-Roasted Butternut Squash 139
Tomatoes:
Almost a Döner Wrap - Mediterranean Style 64
Bee Sting Pizza 96
Cod Stewed with Roasted Tomatoes, Chilis & Olives 123
Eggplant "Meatballs" with Spaghetti 104
Fettuccine with Seared Calamari & Pan Roasted Tomatoes 108
Garlicky Kale Panini with Sweet Tomato Jam, Gruyere & Pancetta 61
Grilled Shrimp Basted with Peach Bourbon BBQ Sauce 126
Hot Eggplant Sandwich with Goat Cheese & a Fried Egg 62
Indian Butter Tofu with Squash & Chickpeas 129
Roasted Cherry, & Butternut Squash Salad with Lime Vinaigrette 50
Smoked Trout, Heirloom Tomato & Whipped Tarragon Goat Cheese Tartine 68
Summertime Plum, Tomato, & Blue Cheese Caprese 44
Tortillas:
Breakfast Tacos with a Kick 38
Chicken Tacos in Cheater's Black Bean Mole 140
Harissa Lamb Quesadillas with Lime Crema 88
Turkey Enchiladas with Maple-Roasted Butternut Squash 139
Trout:
Smoked Trout, Heirloom Tomato & Whipped Tarragon Goat Cheese Tartine 68
Turmeric:
Moroccan Spiced Chicken Pot Pie 133
Spatchcocked Chicken with Orange Turmeric Roasted Brussels & Celery Root 134
Turkey:
Indian Butter Tofu with Squash & Chickpeas 129
Pomegranate Glazed Turkey Meatballs with Baked Basmati Rice 136
Turkey Enchiladas with Maple-Roasted

Butternut Squash 139
Tuna Pâté with Sundried Tomatoes 74

U

Udon Noodles:
Crispy Coconut Fish with Sesame Broccoli & Udon Noodles 116

V

Vanilla Bean:
Cranberry Friand 166
Vermouth:
Autumn Negroni 82
Vodka:
Cherry Ginger Vodka Cooler 87

W

Walnuts:
"Bananas Foster" Sticky Toffee Pudding 164
Overnight French Toast with Pear Maple Syrup 32
Whipped Goat Cheese:
Smoked Trout, Heirloom Tomato & Whipped Tarragon Goat Cheese Tartine 68
Whiskey Soaked Peach Skillet Cake 162
White Beans:
Tuna Pâté with Sundried Tomatoes 74
White Bean & Celery Root Soup with Sausage 58
White Chocolate:
Lime Spiked White Chocolate Macadamia Nut Cookies 144
Wine, Sparkling:
The Hugo 75
Mexican 75 89
Wine, White:
Bay Scallop "Chowder" Pizza 94
Cheesy Baked Asparagus Frittata Topped with Prosciutto 37
Mushroom Leek Soup with Cashew Cream 56
Summertime Aperitivo 78
White Bean & Celery Root Soup with Sausage 58
Yogurt:
Cheesecake Mousse with Roasted Strawberry Puree 158
Chocolate-Chocolate Breakfast Bread 22
Tzatziki 64
Whipped Feta Dip with Mint Chili Oil 72
Zucchini:
Chocolate-Chocolate Breakfast Bread 22
Herby Zucchini Phyllo Pie 98

AUTHORS

Alexis Taylor likes to make the best kind of mess in the kitchen. She enjoys feasts with family and friends, drinking fine wine, and to do it all before 9pm.

Justin Taylor made a deal with his future bride... he'd do the dishes. He smiles every night. In addition to happily serving as a taste tester, he enjoys his roles of photographer, editor, business operations guru and resident mixologist.

CPSIA information can be obtained
at www.ICGtesting.com
Printed in the USA
BVHW021332191021
619299BV00005B/335